DECISIVE BATTLES
OF THE
AMERICAN
REVOLUTION

DECISIVE BATTLES
OF THE
AMERICAN
REVOLUTION

by

Col. Joseph B. Mitchell

MOCKINGBIRD BOOKS

To

SCOTT HART

For a free catalog of
other Mockingbird Books

Write to: MOCKINGBIRD BOOKS
        Box 624
        St. Simons Island, GA 31522

Contents

DECISIVE BATTLES
OF THE
AMERICAN
REVOLUTION

Foreword

THIS book has been written as a companion piece to my book on the Civil War, which attempted to present a short history of the War Between The States with its events and leaders in their proper perspective, placing its battles and campaigns in modern, up-to-date surroundings.

The objectives of this book on the American Revolution have been adopted. The Revolution was first subdivided into phases by selecting the decisive battles of the war. Separate chapters were written to describe the major events occurring in both the North and the South between these limiting dates. Progress maps were prepared to illustrate these chapters. I hope that by this progressive method of discussing the events leading toward a battle, describing the battle itself and then its results, the various events of the war may be kept in their proper place in relation to the whole war effort.

The second objective of this book, to present the battles and campaigns in modern dress by using present-day road maps, presented a much more difficult problem for the Revolution than it did for the Civil War. Not only had the greater passage of time tended to obliterate the roads more thoroughly, but also a greater number of large cities had been established on the battlefield sites. However, since the visitor today can only be guided by what he finds in the area, I decided to use the very latest maps obtainable, plotting thereon the parks, monuments and other new developments. These, taken together with the movements, attack arrows and defensive lines overlaid on the present-day maps, then become aids to understanding what happened. In a few instances, noted in the text, the old roads still appear in the large cities, with perhaps new names, in their original locations.

In some of the battlefield areas, where large cities have not arisen to engulf the battlefield sites, I was surprised to find that many of the old routes can still be traced, and that some of the present-day roads, although paved and straightened in many places, coincide rather closely. These have been indicated insofar as the scale of the map would permit.

I originally designed these maps after a careful study of the terrain. My pencil drawings were then given to Janice Downey who executed them, improving my designs in many ways so that they might present a more attractive and pleasing appearance. The credit for this should be given to her; if any errors are incorporated therein, I am responsible.

Now I hasten to extend belated recognition, and my thanks, to Colonel Charles W. Yuill, my World War II Combat Team Commander, who was the first to suggest the idea of combining on one map the road nets of two different periods of history.

I am very grateful to Colonel William A. Walker and to Colonel John W. McDonald, both of whom I served with on the American Battle Monuments Commission, for their encouragement and their help to me.

Special thanks are due to Miss Lois Dwight Cole, who led me to undertake the preparation of this book and was of great assistance in developing it. I am also indebted to Mr. Charles Dwoskin for helpful criticism and literary advice.

I wish also to take this opportunity to thank my mother, Mrs. William A. Mitchell, for her enthusiasm, confidence and aid, and Miss Emily Johnson for preparing the Index.

Finally I wish to express my appreciation and gratitude to my children, Sherwood and Brad, for their patience and cooperation while this book was being prepared, and to my wife, Vivienne, for her valuable suggestions and for the many hours she spent working with me to complete this project.

J. B. M.

I

The Revolution

THE beginnings and the initial purpose of what came to be known as the War of the American Revolution, or the War for American Independence, have frequently been misstated. John Adams, our second President, once wrote, "The Revolution was effected before the war commenced. The Revolution was in the minds and hearts of the people . . ." This statement, though often quoted, has as often been misunderstood and interpreted to mean that all Americans, by their very heritage, will encourage any fight for freedom. Actually most of our Founding Fathers had no such idea; in fact for a whole year we fought without any Declaration of Independence or general wish for revolution.

It all began almost 170 years before the first shot of the Revolution was fired, with the founding of the colonies themselves. Most of the people who came to this country from Europe fled to avoid some sort of persecution—religious, political or economic—and persecution in those days in Europe was very harsh. Also the concept of the purpose of a colony and the rights of the colonists themselves, was much different from what it is today. For example, England does not tax Canada, Australia and the other members of the British Commonwealth now; they are taxed only by their local parliaments, assemblies or councils.

The first successful British colony had been founded at Jamestown, Virginia, in 1607. Then came the Pilgrims and the Puritans to Massachusetts. Other settlements were established by people of various nationalities, but these were soon brought under British control. Georgia, the last of the thirteen original colonies, was not founded until 1733, but meanwhile the older colonies had expanded rapidly both in population and in area occupied. During this period and in succeeding years the colonists were left alone to a very great extent to develop their own ideas of self-government in their own way. There was very little interference by England. Laws were passed by Parliament concerning taxation and trade but they were not enforced. This negligence was due partly to ignorance of the real and potential resources of the colonies, but the great distance and the time element were also important factors. It usually took over a month for a ship to sail across the Atlantic from England. In addition, during those years England was almost constantly involved in conflict with other nations, particularly France, for supremacy in North America. Four wars were fought in North America with France: King William's War, 1689–1697; Queen Anne's War, 1702–1713; King George's War, 1744–1748; and the French and Indian War, 1754–1763.

The colonies had furnished their quotas of men for those wars and there had been no disloyalty. There had been a good deal of hard feelings because of the contempt shown by the British regulars for their allies of the American militia and the arrogance of the British officers; there had been much discontent because of the billeting of the British troops on the people. But there had been no rupture and the colonies had done about as they pleased. The only real bond to the authority of England was the governors, but they were dependent upon the colonial legislatures for their pay.

The result was that in the freer atmosphere of life in America, far removed from the mother country, the colonists created machinery of self-government and exercised initiative in regulating their affairs and molding their own civilization. They became more self-reliant and independent than would have been possible in the Old World. There grew up on this side of the Atlantic a new people, who although loyal to the British crown, placed quite different interpretations on the British constitution. Furthermore, the change had been so gradual over the years that the King and his ministers, who were not very interested in the colonies anyway during this period, were not aware that it had occurred. The ever-pressing European problems were surely far more important to them than the mental attitude of the colonists in distant America.

Then, after the French and Indian War, the cost of which had been tremendous, King George III and his ministers began to search high and low for ways and means to pay off the enormous public debt. It did not take long for them to discover that the American colonies were a source of revenue.

The first step was a decision to enforce the Navigation Acts which had been on the books for a hundred years but had been consistently evaded. These acts were intended to compel the colonists to export their goods in English ships manned by British crews and to prevent their shipping goods to any but British ports, which was quite in keeping with the European idea of the purpose of forming colonies. This decision came as a shock to the colonists, who were amazed and resentful, and their reaction was a great surprise to King George and his ministers who could see no possible reason for objecting to what they thought was the normal process of government.

Later in 1765 came the Stamp Act which was soon repealed but served during its short life to increase the resentment of the colonists and caused them to raise the cry of "taxation [of the colonies] without representation [in the British Parliament]."

In the succeeding years Parliament passed other acts, all of which were resisted by the colonists. Actually none of them were very burdensome. The government in England considered them to be perfectly natural, since the purpose of founding colonies was to increase the importance of the mother country and provide revenue for those who had financed the undertakings in the first place, and also to help pay for just such things as the cost of the recent French and Indian War.

During these years there were a number of incidents which served to keep both the colonists and the English government aroused. The most important were the Boston Massacre of 1770 in which three citizens were killed and two others mortally wounded, and the Boston Tea Party in 1773. The latter resulted in the passage by Parliament of the "Intolerable Acts," which included the closing of the port of Boston.

When the Boston Port Bill went into effect at noon on June 1, 1774, Lieutenant General Thomas Gage, the military governor, had under his command less than 2,000 troops to enforce the decree. During the next few months his forces slowly but steadily increased until by the beginning of 1775 he had in Boston about 4,000 men of the British Army plus some 450 marines from the ships in the harbor. By April a few other reinforcements had arrived but the total could not have been much over 5,000.

To oppose this army Massachusetts had only its militia, a force which technically included the entire fighting strength of the colony, but a substantial portion of this number were Loyalists. Worcester conceived the idea of having all the officers of its units resign, then new officers were elected to form new units. Here for the first time the idea of the "minutemen" originated. A third of the men were to be appointed to act "at a moment's notice" in any emergency. The idea spread and was adopted by the Massachusetts Provincial Congress in October, 1774. Naturally it took time to organize these units; some were not yet formed by the beginning of the war.

It is most difficult to determine either how many militia or how many minutemen were available by April, 1775. An estimate can be made by noting that immediately after the opening of hostilities Massachusetts resolved to enlist a force of 13,600 men and abandoned the minutemen idea. Thus the system was short-lived, some men serving for only a few days, but at the beginning this hastily organized, untrained group of patriots, equipped with every conceivable type of ancient firearm, proved their worth at Lexington and Concord.

There was certainly no question as to the ability of 5,000 regulars to defeat three times their number of militia on a battlefield, even though some of the colonists had seen service during the French and Indian War and could be counted upon individually as reliable soldiers. Yet this is an oversimplification of the problem facing the British. If Massachusetts rebelled, so might her neighbors. At the same time that the Congress of Massachusetts asked for 13,600 men from her own Commonwealth she resolved to ask for 16,400 more from the rest of the New England colonies, adding up to a total of 30,000 from New England alone.

The population of the thirteen colonies came to about 2,500,000 people as opposed to about 9,000,000 in the British Isles. But England had to provide garrisons for many other far-flung parts of her Empire from India to Africa to Gibraltar. And always in those days she had to be prepared to face her ancient enemies France and Spain who would gladly take the field against her if the opportunity presented itself. Nevertheless, a great deal would certainly be done to ensure that so large a portion of the British Empire as the American colonies did not succeed in a rebellion.

Although it was obviously impossible for General Gage, with only 5,000 regulars, to impose the will of the British Government on the thirteen colonies stretching for over a thousand miles along the Eastern Seaboard, it was also certain that large reinforcements would be sent to him. With these his army could surely take the field and defeat any force that could be brought against him. This seemed especially true when there was no way of properly equipping a colonial force and no time to train it.

In addition and of perhaps greater significance, the Royal Navy, while not in the best of condition owing to the policy of neglect of the armed services which has so often occurred in the history of the English-speaking peoples between wars, was a powerful force. Although its full strength could not be employed against America so long as there was the possibility of France and Spain intervening, whatever strength was used would have complete control of the sea. The colonists had no navy at all.

So the British Army could be transported to and landed along the Eastern Seaboard and conduct operations inland. Of course it would take some months for convoys to arrive from the old country, but this fact was counterbalanced by the conditions of the roads in the colonies, which were few and far between and generally in poor condition. Any army which the colonists could possibly raise to defend their shores against attack would have a most difficult time, not only in guessing where the blow would fall but also in assembling at that point to meet it.

Thus, although General Gage's army in Boston was inadequate, it could be increased to a substantial size within a few months' time if the necessity arose. General Gage appears to have hoped that war would not come. Although many of the colonists, especially those living in Boston, would have refused to believe it, he appears to have been a friend of the colonies. He had come to America many years previously, had served in the French and Indian War, had taken part in the disastrous Braddock expedition, and later had seen action in other battles and campaigns. In addition he was married to an American girl of a prominent New Jersey family, had been on friendly terms with many colonial leaders, and owned land in New York.

General Gage's own experience, as well as that of many other British officers, must have told him that the capture of one of America's larger cities would not be the end of a campaign. America's strength lay not in her large industrial cities, of which there were none, but in the farms and along the frontiers. One of the greatest problems facing the colonial leaders would be somehow to obtain guns and ammunition which they could not manufacture for themselves in any quantity. Also, in addition to the lack of industrial capacity, there was no economic stability; in fact the colonists who led this revolt seem to have started with almost nothing.

Of these facts the colonial leaders were certainly well aware. In addition it was difficult to get the thirteen colonies to act together. Not only were they separated by many miles of poor roads and inadequate transportation facilities, they were composed of such diverse elements as the Pilgrims and Puritans who had fled to New England so that they could worship God in their own way, the Dutch and Swedish, French Huguenots, Cavaliers, Quakers, Roman Catholics, fortune seekers and former inmates of debtors' prisons. The people of New York and Pennsylvania distrusted the Yankees from New England, who in turn were suspicious of them and also of the southerners from Maryland, Delaware and other states farther south who disliked the strait-laced Yankees and regarded them with a certain amount of contempt.

With such a mixture of peoples there was no unanimity

of opinion, even after the shooting started. At the beginning the majority were not seeking independence; they simply wanted to be granted the rights they thought British subjects should have. The most important of these rights was that of governing themselves through their elected legislative assemblies which had been established in one form or another in each of the colonies. This was extremely difficult for King George and his ministers to understand since the people of England did not have a truly representative government. However, many of the leaders of the British Whig party, opposed to the Tories then in power in England, recognized that the Americans were fighting for the same principles that they were striving for in Great Britain, and consistently supported the American point of view in Parliament. In fact the success of the Revolution can be considered as a part of the long battle of Englishmen for liberty, although the reforms which made Parliament a completely representative body did not come about until the nineteenth century.

From a military aspect this lack of enthusiasm in England was important because many officers of the British Army resigned rather than fight the Americans, and it was also one of the factors which led to the hiring of German mercenary soldiers to help put down the rebellion. The employment of these foreigners was bitterly resented by the colonists and hastened the passage of the Declaration of Independence.

With sentiment divided in England, it was only natural to find varying degrees of intensity of feeling in America. Some colonies contained a much larger number of people loyal to the King than did others, and included among these were many of the most influential civic and business leaders. It has been estimated that only about one half of the people were actively in favor of the war; the remainder were either indifferent or fought for the King. A number of regiments were composed of Loyalists who fought effectively on the British side. The American Revolution was no exception to the general rule that the people in a rebellious country are divided in sentiment and end by fighting each other, and that where this occurs battles are often savage and bitterly contested.

II

From Lexington to Bunker Hill

DURING the months preceding actual conflict the patriots of Massachusetts made every effort to collect ammunition and other supplies. This was not a simple problem. Some powder and ball was available to them, having been acquired in the normal course of events because of their militia status, but this was strictly limited. A small amount was also obtained by smuggling. But the prime, and most obvious, sources were the British stores in various places along the coast. These were usually guarded only by small caretaking detachments.

This situation was of course known to both the patriots and the British, who simultaneously made efforts to either reinforce the garrisons concerned or to first remove the supplies themselves. Numerous clashes resulted throughout the six months preceding the beginning of the war itself. None of these skirmishes were of great importance but they served to fan the fires of rebellion.

What few supplies the patriots did acquire were stored under guard at various strategic points throughout the colony. One of the more important of these was situated at Concord, only eighteen miles by road from Boston.

On April 15, 1775, the British grenadiers and light

infantrymen in Boston were relieved from all their normal duties for special training. This news spread rapidly through the city; certainly something was going to happen soon, for these were supposed to be the best soldiers of their regiments, selected for outstanding qualities.

A British regiment at the time of the Revolution was composed of ten companies. The total strength was supposed to be about 475 men, but they were often short of personnel and usually averaged less than 400 men during the war. Of these ten companies, one was a light-infantry company whose members were chosen for physical agility, alertness and vigor. They were used for reconnaissance, skirmishing, and protecting the flanks of the army while on the march. The other elite company of each regiment was the grenadier company—the shock troops—the tallest and strongest men of the regiment. On many occasions the grenadiers and light infantrymen from several regiments were grouped together into battalions for special purposes such as leading assault columns on key objectives, flank marches, river crossings, or defense of critical areas.

Therefore when these soldiers were relieved from their regular duties for some unannounced purpose the residents of Boston immediately became suspicious. They correctly guessed that the British were preparing to march on Concord. The only question was whether the troops would go all the way by land via Boston Neck, or be rowed across the Charles River to the north bank and move to Concord by that route. Paul Revere made arrangements for lanterns to be hung in the steeple of the Old North Church as a signal to waiting couriers: one lantern would signal the British had marched by land; two lanterns would mean they were crossing the river, i.e., going by sea.

On the afternoon of April 18 General Gage sent out mounted officers to patrol the roads and try to prevent the people from hearing of the expedition. About 10:30

P.M. some 800 troops under the command of Lieutenant Colonel Francis Smith quietly assembled and began embarking in their boats.

Dr. Joseph Warren immediately sent William Dawes and then Paul Revere to Lexington to warn John Hancock and Samuel Adams of danger. Taking the longer route via Boston Neck and evading the British guards stationed there, Dawes rode toward Lexington alerting the countryside. Revere had two lanterns hung in the Old North Church, then was rowed across the river to Charlestown, and began his famous midnight ride. Seeing the signal, other riders soon began spreading the word.

Paul Revere reached Lexington first, awakened John Hancock and Samuel Adams, then waited for Dawes. Together they rode on toward Concord, were joined by Dr. Samuel Prescott, then were intercepted by British officers. Dawes got away, but although Revere and Prescott were captured, Prescott escaped and brought the word to Concord.

The minutemen immediately began to assemble. The first clash occurred at Lexington where a group of about seventy gathered on the village green early in the morning of April 19 to await the arrival of the troops. It is difficult to understand what they expected to accomplish against such superior numbers. However, their leader, Captain John Parker, cautioned them not to fire unless fired upon, but said, "If war is to come, let it begin here."

Soon the leading British troops appeared, six companies of light infantry commanded by Major John Pitcairn, an officer of the Royal Marines. He promptly formed them on the village green facing the minutemen and commanded the rebels to disperse. Reluctantly they began to do so in small groups, when someone fired a shot. Who fired the first "shot heard round the world" at Lexington on April 19, 1775, is not known. Nor is it certain whether he was British or American; each side claimed the other fired first. The weight of evidence makes it appear probable that a British soldier fired against orders, but it is entirely immaterial who pulled the trigger. The war, which lasted for eight long years before the hostilities officially ceased, was bound to come sooner or later at Lexington or some other place.

As a result of this so-called battle, eight minutemen were killed and ten wounded, while one of the British soldiers was also wounded, and Pitcairn's horse was hit. The column then marched onward to Concord.

When they arrived the British found that most of the supplies had already been removed or hidden. This had been done as a result of the advance warning, under the direction of Colonel James Barrett who was in general command of the militia in this district. While the troops were engaged in searching the town of Concord, Lieutenant Colonel Smith posted several outguards to provide warning of and prevent any attack by the minutemen. One of these outposts across the Concord River was attacked by minutemen and forced to retreat. The British then began their historic retreat to Boston.

This return march was not to be a triumphal one. By this time the countryside was thoroughly aroused. The patriots swarmed to the scene from all directions, shooting at the enemy from fences and hedgerows as they passed. Although the British Light Infantry, moving on the flanks, continued to clear these snipers out of the way, losses mounted and the retreat began to assume the appearance of a rout. The only thing that saved the column was an additional body of some 900 troops which General Gage had sent out to meet them under the command of Lord Percy. Covered by these fresh troops, the disorganized column managed to reach Boston. The total British casualties for the day amounted to 273, while the Americans suffered only 95.

Thus began the longest war in the history of what was to become the United States of America. So far it had involved only Massachusetts, but now, at the call of

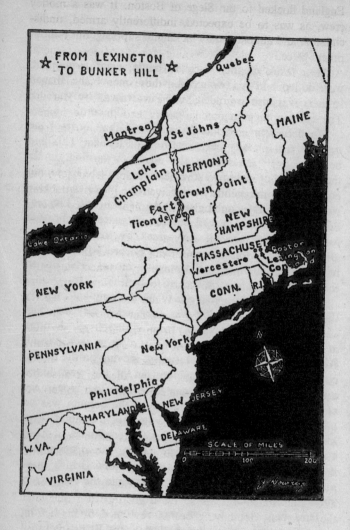

that colony, thousands of militia from all over New England flocked to the Siege of Boston. It was a motley crew, as was to be expected, indifferently armed, undisciplined, and almost totally lacking in supplies, but temporarily effective as a besieging force. Major General Artemas Ward, appointed by Massachusetts to command, was hard put to it even to feed these men but managed somehow. In the first few days he was saved by Harvard University which opened its doors and its food lockers to the hungry men. Later, food began to come in from the surrounding country and from neighboring colonies, not in quantity but sufficient to survive.

During this period two American leaders separately, but practically simultaneously, conceived the idea of attacking Fort Ticonderoga on Lake Champlain in New York. Benedict Arnold, a captain of Connecticut Militia, was commissioned by the Massachusetts Committee of Safety as a colonel to form a force for this purpose. In Vermont, Ethan Allen, commissioned colonel by Connecticut, gathered together some of the men from the New Hampshire Grants for the same purpose. When the two met, Allen's Green Mountain Boys were ready but Arnold's men had not yet arrived on the scene. From the first the two men disliked each other intensely and argued vehemently about who would be in command. With his militia present and Arnold's absent, Ethan Allen of course became the commander, although he consented to let Arnold remain at his side.

Together in the early morning of May 10, 1775, with 83 men, they rushed the gates of the fort and overpowered the small 50-man garrison. Ethan Allen announced to the startled commander that he was acting by the authority of "The Great Jehovah and the Continental Congress." The latter statement was so far from the truth that later the Congress, not having been forewarned of his action, seriously debated returning the fort to the British because the colonies were not in revolt. At that time the majority were still attempting to avoid actual rebellion, hoping to obtain a peaceful settlement of their grievances and remain loyal subjects of the Crown.

Two days after the capture of Fort Ticonderoga (which was originally built by the French in 1756 and has now been completely restored), Lieutenant Colonel Seth Warner seized Crown Point. Colonel Arnold then took St. Johns, subsequently abandoned it, and the post was promptly retaken by the British.

Meanwhile in Virginia, which next to Massachusetts was the state most disposed to rebellion, the Royal Governor, Lord Dunmore, fled to the safety of a British man-of-war at Yorktown. He was one of the worst of the royal governors and had even threatened to arm the slaves in order to put down a rebellion.

The settlers in Kentucky had been under Indian attack on the frontier even before the shooting at Lexington and Concord. News of the beginning of the war between the whites was sufficient to cause the Indians to intensify their assaults upon the settlers. Also at this time in New York the Americans and the British were competing with each other for Indian aid. Here the key figure was Colonel Guy Johnson, the Superintendent of Indian Affairs, and he was definitely pro-British.

On June 14, 1775, the Continental Congress in Philadelphia passed a resolution authorizing the formation of a Continental Army. This date is now observed as the birthday of the United States Army although the act authorized only 10 companies of expert riflemen, 6 in Pennsylvania, 2 in Maryland and 2 in Virginia.

On June 15 John Adams offered another resolution. It was that Colonel George Washington of the Virginia militia be appointed general and commander in chief, a position which he accepted the next day.

It is doubtful if the Congress throughout its existence performed any other acts of greater importance to the future of the United States. In the coming years the

Continental Army, although usually underpaid or not paid at all and always far under authorized strength, was to provide the only regulars the colonies ever had. Without these troops the Revolution could never have been won. They became the dependable trained nucleus around which the militia formed, the steadying influence in every major battle in which they participated.

The selection of General Washington as commander in chief was undoubtedly the wisest possible choice. It is said that John Hancock, the presiding officer of the Congress, was offended because he was not chosen, but he had the good sense to eventually realize that Washington was far better trained than he and a more logical choice for several reasons. In the first place the new commander, although not a trained soldier, had seen an unusual amount of combat service in the French and Indian War. He was well known throughout the colonies as a gentleman of outstanding character, completely honest, not a political agitator but one who firmly believed in the justice of the colonial cause. Everyone in the Congress knew him to be a leader in whom they could put absolute trust. Later there would be intrigues against him, but it is doubtful if there was another man in the colonies who could have held the army together throughout the dark and trying times to come. Certainly there was none who could have done it as well.

The Congress also appointed certain other generals at the same time. Artemas Ward, already in command of the men around Boston, was naturally chosen as the senior major general. Next in rank was Charles Lee. He had been an officer in the British Army and had also served as a soldier of fortune in various parts of the world and was supposed to be well trained and gifted in his profession. It was expected that he would serve as a capable adviser on military matters to the commander in chief.

The other major generals chosen were Philip Schuyler

and Israel Putnam. The brigadiers elected were: Seth Pomeroy, Richard Montgomery, David Wooster, William Heath, Joseph Spencer, John Thomas, John Sullivan and Nathanael Greene. In addition Horatio Gates, another former British officer like Lee, was chosen adjutant general with the rank of brigadier.

General Washington promptly started for Boston but before he had ridden more than twenty miles he received news of a battle that had taken place there on June 17.

III

The Battle of Bunker Hill

IN 1775 Boston was a city of about 16,000 people and was situated on a peninsula with a very narrow neck of land at its base. To the north across the Charles River was the village of Charlestown on the south side of another peninsula which was also joined to the mainland by a very narrow neck. (The city has grown so much and the rivers and harbor have been so filled by land that the shore line of today only faintly resembles that at the time of the Revolution. Both Boston Neck and Charlestown Neck have been widened to several times their original widths.)

General Gage had insured the safety of the city of Boston from attack by land by the simple process of fortifying Boston Neck, but artillery emplaced on the hills on the Charlestown peninsula would be a definite threat to the city. The same was true of the hills on Dorchester Heights (South Boston) which were on a third but much wider peninsula to the south.

General Gage had now received reinforcements. With them had also come three other British officers all of whom were destined to play prominent parts in the Revolution: Major Generals William Howe, John Burgoyne and Henry Clinton. The arrival of these three on the frigate *Cerberus* (named for the three-headed dog supposed to guard the entrance to the infernal regions) was the subject of many a jest.

In any event General Gage and his colleagues decided to seize Dorchester Heights. Word of the plan reached the colonists, who determined to forestall the British by occupying and fortifying Bunker Hill on the Charlestown peninsula. On the night of June 16, 1775, they quietly moved forward and started to build a redoubt on Breed's Hill rather than Bunker Hill, because although it was somewhat lower it was nearer to Boston. Auxiliary defenses were to be erected on Bunker Hill. The battle which followed on June 17 should have been called Breed's Hill, not Bunker Hill. (The granite monument 221 feet high stands within the lines of the American Redoubt which was the center of the battle.)

Colonel William Prescott appears to have been the man who decided to fortify Breed's Hill. This was done with General Putnam's consent and was a correct decision since the hillsides were steeper and therefore easier to defend against a bayonet charge which was the primary threat and weapon of the infantry of those days. Today we are taught to use fire and movement, but that assumes that the fire delivered can be accurate and effective. However, the musket of the Revolution was completely unreliable. If it fired at all when the trigger was pulled, there was a long wait while the powder flashed in the pan; the bullet was heavy and caused a terrific shoulder concussion; there was no rear sight because the bullets were not accurate beyond perhaps eighty yards. The standard method of attack was to fire a few, maybe only one or two, volleys at the defenders, then charge with the bayonet. The British were supremely good at this and had proved it on countless European battlefields.

When a British ship discovered the redoubt being erected by the Americans on the morning of June 17, it promptly opened fire upon it, awakening everyone within miles including General Gage who immediately determined to eject the patriots from those hills. Gage entrusted the job to General Howe.

The task should and could have been simple. While the warships in the harbor, which were already shelling the rebel position, continued their fire, the troops could be embarked in boats and moved behind and to the west of the hills where the neck narrowed, and thus cut the rebels off from retreat. A landing near the end of the peninsula was determined upon instead. It has been said that this decision was made because British army officers at that time were completely disdainful of the militia and were determined to show that it was not at all necessary to honor them by employing proper military tactics. A frontal attack delivered against this rabble would be the more effective because it would show the utter invincibility of the British Army and the uselessness of attempting to oppose it. This legend is not entirely true, because General Clinton actually advised an attack against the Charlestown Neck but was overruled.

General Howe moved his troops by rowboat to the Charlestown peninsula and when all was ready launched his assault. The result proved, if any further proof were necessary to add to the long record of history, that the one thing untrained troops can do if properly led, besides sniping from ambush, is to hold their ground against direct attack when sheltered by fortifications.

Our history books make much of the fact that the British delivered a direct assault upon the American Redoubt. This is true but it was not planned that way at all. A secondary assault was initially launched along the beach to outflank the Americans on their left and to get behind them. At this point Colonel John Stark with his New Hampshire soldiers, and Captain Thomas Knowlton with a few troops from Connecticut, had erected a stone and rail fence as a barrier down to the water's edge; it

THE BATTLE OF
BUNKER HILL

— American Positions,
June 17, 1775
← British Attacks,
June 17, 1775

was here that the initial attack came. When it was re-pulsed the main assault under the command of Major General Howe and Brigadier General Sir Robert Pigot followed.

So much has been written about the bravery and courage of the New England farmers who faced the Brit-ish that a word about General Howe, who personally led the main assault, would not be out of place. In 1759 he had distinguished himself by personally leading the first twenty-four men up the Plains of Abraham, which re-sulted in Wolfe's victory over Montcalm at Quebec. He proved his courage again in this battle.

Two notable Americans who came on the scene just before the battle as volunteers should also be mentioned. They were Joseph Warren who had been appointed a major general but had not yet received his commission, and General Seth Pomeroy, seventy years old, carrying the musket which he had used at Louisbourg in King George's War thirty years before. Both men refused command and served as private soldiers.

When the attack came the defenders, following the command not to shoot until "you see the whites of their eyes," held their fire, then blasted the oncoming attackers with a withering volley at close range. Many people have written about the accuracy of American fire delivered from rifles by men trained in their use from boyhood. It does not apply here. These men were not backwoodsmen, and there was probably not a single rifle in their posses-sion. It was simple, massed musketry fire that repelled the attack.

Stunned, the British fell back, but with the characteris-tic courage of the British soldier, rallied and renewed the attack. It was not until the third assault, however, when Howe had received reinforcements including General Clinton who had crossed from Boston to help, that the militia, their ammunition gone, were forced backward off the hill, still fighting with clubbed muskets. They had little chance against the bayonet.

In this battle the Americans, out of some 3,200 engaged, suffered about 440 casualties, including Joseph Warren who lost his life. Most of the casualties occurred in the retreat, which is to be expected. There were probably never more than 1,500 engaged at one time. There was little co-ordination between the Americans involved. With trained troops General Putnam could have counterattacked from Bunker Hill instead of waiting to be driven from Bunker Hill too.

The British of course suffered greater casualties than the Americans—about 1,500 out of 2,400 engaged. The lesson was not lost on General Howe who never again engaged in a series of costly frontal assaults. Unfortunately, however, it also encouraged the idea that Americans did not need to be trained to fight.

IV

From Bunker Hill to the Evacuation of Boston

NOT all of the Americans involved in the Battle of Bunker Hill fought as well as those defending the hills. Certain units ordered forward to support the position either lost their way or never attempted to execute their orders. When Washington arrived on the scene and took command of the militia he found many grave weaknesses which took him months to correct; incompetent officers elected to command, undisciplined troops, unsanitary campsites—from the very first Washington's patience was taxed to the limit.

There were a few exceptions. The most notable was the encampment of the Rhode Island brigade which appeared neat and orderly. The commander was Brigadier General Nathanael Greene, a Quaker who was promptly expelled from his church when he offered his sword to the service of his colony.

When he arrived, General Washington found himself confronted with the double task of trying to train his militia and also enlist as many as possible in the Continental Army. This was a slow, heartbreaking process. He could try to persuade the men to join and set an example for them, but he could not stoop to curry favor with them as so many of the elected officers had done.

In July and August the newly formed companies of expert riflemen of the Continental Army arrived on the scene. One of these was commanded by Captain Daniel Morgan who was to distinguish himself in the years to come. The arrival of these units helped to spur enlistments to a certain extent but most of the militia were intent upon returning home as soon as possible even if it meant leaving the field of battle. The most horrible example, however, did not occur in front of Boston but in the Canadian woods far to the north.

Many American colonists, especially those in New England, feared an invasion from Canada. Others believed that their neighbors to the north felt the same as they did and would join them if given the chance. An expedition was planned to capture Montreal and Quebec and drive the British from Canadian soil. The advance northward would be made in two widely separated columns converging upon Quebec.

The first column, under Brigadier General Richard Montgomery, was to move via Fort Ticonderoga and Lake Champlain, seize Montreal, then proceed eastward down the St. Lawrence to Quebec. The second column, under the command of Colonel Benedict Arnold, was to proceed up the Kennebec River to Maine, thence across the uncharted wilderness to join Montgomery at Quebec.

Of the two tasks, the column from New York had the easier, although it was opposed by a few scattered British troops and some Canadian militia. General Montgomery began his advance northward on August 28, 1775, with some 1,200 men. General Schuyler, in command of the New York Department, joined him a week later with 700 more. After several unsuccessful attempts to take the British fort at St. Johns, Schuyler became sick and was forced to leave. General Montgomery carried on and eventually took St. Johns, then entered Montreal on

November 13. In the meantime Ethan Allen had managed to get himself captured in a daring but foolish venture. Always impatient and contemptuous of higher authority, he had attempted, with an entirely inadequate force, to take Montreal by surprise. The result was definitely harmful to the American cause because it encouraged the Canadians who were loyal to the crown.

Although the British commander, Major General Guy Carleton, Military Governor of Canada, conducted a skillful defense with the few troops available to him, he was forced steadily backward. But it was getting to be wintertime and only a few Canadians had come to join the invading force. The situation was ominous; it seemed the height of folly to proceed toward Quebec through this unfriendly country in the winter, but Montgomery was committed to make every effort to meet Arnold at Quebec.

In the meantime Arnold was having more than his share of trouble. There was no enemy opposition but his boats had proved unserviceable. Supplies were running short; many were lost when boats were swamped or sank. The weather was miserably cold and rainy. Then snow began to fall. Some of Arnold's men chose to desert under the leadership of faint-hearted officers, taking precious food with them. The march became a nightmare, men pressing forward blindly with practically no hope of survival. But under the energetic leadership of Colonel Arnold, Lieutenant Colonel Christopher Greene, Captain Morgan and a few other intrepid souls, the troops kept going until finally on November 9, after two months of almost incredible suffering, they reached the shores of the St. Lawrence opposite Quebec. Six hundred men came through out of the 1,100 who had started on this historic march, one of the most famous in military history.

Colonel Arnold might have captured Quebec out of hand; it was very lightly garrisoned. But a storm arose which prevented his crossing the river, and reinforcements slipped into the city. By November 13, when the storm

FROM BUNKER HILL
☆ TO THE ☆
EVACUATION OF BOSTON

Quebec

MAINE

Montreal   St Johns

St Lawrence   Kennebec

Lake Champlain   VERMONT

Portland (Felmouth)

Fort Ticonderoga   NEW HAMPSHIRE

Lake Ontario

MASSACHUSETTS
Boston

NEW YORK   CONN.   R.I.

PENNSYLVANIA   New York

Philadelphia   NEW JERSEY

MARYLAND   DELAWARE

W. VA.   SCALE OF MILES

0   100   200

VIRGINIA

OHIO PENNSYLVANIA MARYLAND NEW JERSEY DELAWARE

WEST VIRGINIA

VIRGINIA

Norfolk

NORTH CAROLINA

Moore's Creek Bridge

Wilmington

N

SOUTH CAROLINA

Charleston

GEORGIA

Savannah

FROM BUNKER HILL
☆ TO THE ☆
EVACUATION OF BOSTON

SCALE OF MILES
0   100   200

FLORIDA

had abated, General Carleton had available a mixed
crew of soldiers, marines, sailors and about 500 militia,
totalling about 1,200 men. The only thing Arnold could
do was wait for Montgomery who arrived on December
2 with only 300 men, but he did have artillery and
clothing. En route he had managed to capture a whole
year's supply of winter uniforms which had been in
storage for the use of two British regiments. The Americans began a siege of Quebec. But time was running out.
The enlistments of most of the men were due to expire
at the end of the year. They had been willing to undergo
the terrible ordeal of reaching Quebec and would continue
to fight until midnight December 31, but could not be
persuaded to stay longer to complete the job that they
had come so far to do.

As a last resort the American leaders decided to make
a night assault upon the city's fortifications. Although they
had about 1,100 men now, Carleton had about 1,800.
Two columns were to converge upon the city that night
but a blizzard arose, the task proved impossible, and the
attack failed. General Montgomery was killed, Arnold
was seriously wounded, and Greene and Morgan were
captured, to be exchanged at a later date. All hope of
success was gone. The best that Colonel Arnold could
possibly do was to retreat some distance to the west and
try to hold what he had gained. By the middle of March,
Arnold, now a brigadier general, had received a few reinforcements, but most of his command was ill with
smallpox, and supplies of all sorts were lacking. The out-
look was dismal indeed, but Arnold was still there. The
Canadian venture would soon die but it was not quite
dead yet.

Meanwhile in front of Boston, Washington was also
having little success with his enlistment problems and a
great deal of trouble with the militia officers, many of
whom he had to cashier for incompetence. For a long time
the siege was only a gigantic bluff. If the British had

chosen to attack, Washington could not have hoped to stop them, but no such effort was made.

Throughout this period Washington also fully appreciated the fact that his siege was not complete. So long as the Royal Navy controlled the seas and the entrance to the harbor, the enemy could continue to supply the garrison and withdraw it at will at any time. The colonials, with no heavy guns available, could not shell the port, nor did they have any means of seizing command of the adjacent waters. On his own initiative Washington commissioned a few privateers to harass the enemy commerce. These were fairly successful in some instances and caused the enemy the loss of a few ships. They certainly annoyed Admiral Samuel Graves, the British naval commander, who reacted by burning the town of Falmouth, now Portland, Maine, on October 16, 1775. Down in Virginia, Lord Dunmore celebrated New Year's Day, 1776, by bombarding, from the safety of his ships, the city of Norfolk, one of Virginia's principal seaports, and burning four-fifths of the city.

As New Year's Day dawned in front of Boston, Washington found that he had so few enlisted men that he had to call on the militia to help maintain the siege. Slowly, however, things improved so that he eventually outnumbered the British. He still had no cannon but that problem was solved during the winter by his chief of artillery, Colonel Henry Knox, a former bookseller by trade. With much hard work and tireless exertion he and his men managed to drag all the way from Boston, by oxcart and through the snow, many of the guns captured at Fort Ticonderoga. At last Washington had the means at hand to force an evacuation of the city.

The newly acquired guns could be mounted on Bunker and Breed's Hills and shell the city from there, but a position on that long, narrow neck of land would still be vulnerable to an attack from the rear. A far better position was on Dorchester Heights to the south from which cannon could dominate the port. As the morning of March 5, 1776, dawned, the British awoke to find those hills in the possession of the rebels who were fortifying themselves and their gun emplacements. After one abortive attempt to move troops across the water to attack this new position—which was frustrated by a gale—the British decided to evacuate Boston. On Saint Patrick's Day General Howe, who had some months before succeeded Gage and who was now a lieutenant general with the local rank of full general in command of all the British troops, sailed out of the harbor to Halifax, Nova Scotia. He took with him all of the Loyalists and their families.

While these events were taking place neither the patriots nor the Loyalists had been idle in the Carolinas and Georgia. Here, however, there were no large armies facing each other. Small bands who fought viciously were formed in each colony. Because of the small numbers of the forces involved the engagements were very personal and bitter. The most important was the Battle of Moore's Creek Bridge, which was fought near Wilmington on February 27, 1776, and resulted in a victory for the colonists and control of most of North Carolina. It was especially important at this time because a joint expedition under the command of General Henry Clinton and Admiral Sir Peter Parker was already en route for the southern theater and had expected to co-operate with those same Loyalists in North Carolina.

V

From the Evacuation of Boston to the Battles Around New York

THE British strategic plan for 1776 was threefold. There were to be two attacks in the north and one in the south. The main effort in the north would take advantage of the long, almost uninterrupted waterway stretching from New York City up the Hudson then via Lake George and Lake Champlain to Canada. The main British army would land at New York while another army would push south from Canada, thus separating New England from the rest of the other colonies. The secondary effort in the south was to seize some of the major cities and control these colonies with the aid of the many Loyalists whom the British expected to find there.

Washington's problem, with the main American army under his control, was to guess accurately where the point of attack would come, so that preparations could be made to meet it. He correctly divined that it would be New York, a city of approximately 25,000 people, the largest seaport on the coast. Promptly after the evacuation of Boston he moved the army to defend that area.

However, although the force to attack the southern theater was already en route, the first British blow was struck in Canada in May when General John Burgoyne

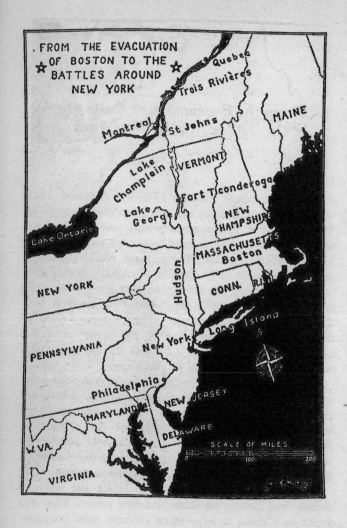

FROM THE EVACUATION OF BOSTON TO THE BATTLES AROUND NEW YORK

Quebec

Trois Rivières

Montreal

St Johns

MAINE

Lake Champlain

VERMONT

Fort Ticonderoga

NEW HAMPSHIRE

Lake George

Lake Ontario

MASSACHUSETTS
Boston

NEW YORK

Hudson

CONN.

R.I.

Long Island

PENNSYLVANIA

New York

Philadelphia

NEW JERSEY

MARYLAND

DELAWARE

W. VA.

VIRGINIA

SCALE OF MILES
0   100   200

OHIO
PENNSYLVANIA
MARYLAND
NEW JERSEY
DELAWARE
WEST VIRGINIA
VIRGINIA
NORTH CAROLINA
Moore's Creek Bridge.
Wilmington
SOUTH CAROLINA
Charleston
GEORGIA
Savannah
FLORIDA

FROM THE
EVACUATION OF BOSTON
☆ TO THE BATTLES ☆
AROUND NEW YORK

SCALE OF MILES
0   100   200

J. Sweeney

arrived with a large army and the garrison sallied forth to attack the half-starved, smallpox-ridden Americans. General John Thomas, then in command, Arnold having withdrawn after being injured by a fall from his horse, had no choice but to retreat. En route Thomas and many of his men died of the smallpox. In spite of this, when some reinforcements arrived the Americans made a final effort at the Battle of Trois Rivières (Three Rivers) on June 8, but were defeated by superior numbers. July found them back again at Fort Ticonderoga.

Meanwhile in May, General Henry Clinton's force had met Sir Peter Parker's fleet with General Charles Cornwallis commanding the troops on board, off the coast of North Carolina. Finding that the Battle of Moore's Creek Bridge had deprived them of any help from the Loyalists of North Carolina, they sailed for Charleston. This city of 12,000 population, the largest in the south, was of course a fairly logical point of attack.

Command of the southern theater had been given to General Charles Lee who arrived in the Charleston area about the same time the British fleet did early in June, and began preparations to defend the city. Immediately a difference of opinion arose. Prior to Lee's arrival, South Carolina soldiers had begun construction of Fort Sullivan on Sullivan's Island in the harbor. It was built of palmetto logs resting on a dirt embankment, and General Lee considered it practically worthless. After all the work that had gone into its construction, he made it clear that he thought it should be abandoned, but the South Carolinians refused. Never a tactful man, Lee quickly made a number of enemies among the people he had come to help. Thus the defending forces were split into two factions, each making its own preparations to conduct a defense along two entirely different lines.

The little fort in the harbor became the center of attention when the British fleet opened fire upon it on June 28. General Clinton had previously landed a large force on an adjacent island. He expected that after the guns of the fort had been silenced by the navy this force would wade across the interval between the two islands and storm the fort.

From the very beginning the British plan went wrong. The spongy palmetto logs did not break apart but actually seemed to absorb the shock of the heavy cannon balls. Colonel William Moultrie and his brave garrison continued to fire back in spite of the hail of shot and shell flying around their heads, and inflicted far more damage than they received. Admiral Sir Peter Parker found himself personally involved when a round shot tore or blew off most of his breeches. The army commander, General Clinton, looked on helplessly while his landing force discovered that the water between the islands across which it was supposed to wade was seven feet deep. The expedition ended in utter failure. Over two years were to pass before the British made another major effort to invade the south. Fort Sullivan was renamed Fort Moultrie in honor of Colonel Moultrie and his gallant men.

On the sea the British continued from time to time to lose a few vessels to American privateers. In October, 1775, the Continental Congress had voted funds for a small fleet of ships. Under the command of Commodore Esek Hopkins they had sailed from the Delaware in mid-February, 1776, bound for Nassau in the Bahamas where a quantity of powder was known to be stored. On March 3 they captured these valuable munitions and then succeeded in bringing them safely to New London. The next month Lieutenant John Barry, commanding the brig *Lexington,* captured the first British naval ship ever taken by the American navy. (In 1954 the United States Government erected a monument to his memory at his birthplace, Weymouth, Ireland.) These were small beginnings for our navy, but auspicious ones.

VI

The Battles Around New York

ON July 4, 1776, the Declaration of Independence was signed. To many it may have seemed a propitious time. The colonials had been successful in almost all their endeavors. There was no longer any large British force on American soil. Howe had evacuated Boston, New England was free, and soon came the news of the victory at Charleston. The only real defeats suffered by the colonists had occurred far away in Canada, and yet upper New York State was still in American hands. One example of the public reaction when the news of the Declaration spread throughout the colonies occurred in New York City. In great excitement the citizens tore down the bronze equestrian statue of George III in Bowling Green, an act which Washington later mildly denounced, but no one who believed in independence could possibly conceal his feelings now that the great step had been taken.

It is probable that only a few individuals fully realized how long a struggle lay ahead. England had not yet committed a large force to battle. There were still several thousand active Loyalists scattered throughout the colonies, and no way had yet been found to supply and equip whatever troops the colonies might call to arms.

The situation was forcibly brought to the attention of the citizens of New York City and of nearby New Jersey towns only eight days after the Declaration when on July 12 the main British fleet of 150 warships and transports appeared to join the 130 ships already present off Staten Island. When the fleet carrying Clinton's troops sailed back from Charleston and still more ships and men arrived, the invading army numbered 32,000 men. It was an unusually large force for that era, by far the largest ever assembled on the North American continent, and it was escorted by an extremely powerful naval force including several ships of the line which correspond to the battleships of today. The fleet was commanded by General Howe's elder brother, Vice Admiral Viscount Richard Howe, known as "Black Dick" because of his swarthy complexion.

It had not been an easy matter for England to gather together such a large number of troops to send to America. There were so many other garrisons to maintain in other parts of the world that King George III had decided to employ foreign mercenaries. His first request for such troops had been made to Catherine the Great of Russia who had refused to furnish any. He had then turned to various German princes who had agreed to send the required numbers. So a large percentage of the British army facing New York City was composed of German soldiers, most of whom came from Hesse-Cassel. Apparently the King saw nothing wrong with this practice. It was not new in European history; mercenary soldiers had enlisted in foreign armies for hundreds of years, but the Americans resented it bitterly. They felt that if the King of England saw fit to hire Hessians to fight against Americans it was yet further proof, if any had been needed, of his contempt and scorn of the patriots and their cause.

Although the British occupied Staten Island, they made no other offensive moves for more than a month. The

Howe brothers were both members of the Whig party which had for years opposed the King and the Tories, and thus they had been favorably inclined and sympathetic toward the colonial cause. In addition, the King had given the Howes authority to pardon the colonists. It would appear that the reason for their long delay on this and on many other occasions in the future was that they hoped it would not be necessary to completely defeat and destroy the Americans. They seemed to think that a show of force or a partial victory on their part would be a better way to induce the patriots to stop fighting and would cause less hard feeling in the future when the colonists again became loyal subjects of the Crown.

It is difficult to explain in any other way the long intervals that occurred between the battles around New York and the lack of effective pursuit when the British did win a battle. For General Howe was a well-trained, experienced soldier and had proved his ability over many years of service. He would do so again in the battles to come, but only apparently when he chose to act; in between times he would let golden opportunities slip through his fingers.

The Howe brothers' first attempts to open a correspondence with Washington were almost ludicrous. If they addressed letters to him as "General Washington" they would be partially recognizing the existence of the young republic. Their first letters addressed to "Mr. Washington" and to "George Washington, Esq., etc.," were politely but firmly refused. They argued that "etc.," covered everything; Washington stated that it could mean "anything." This correspondence continued during the intervals between battles and led to meetings of commissioners from each side. Of course these meetings came to naught because the Howes had been given no authority to discuss the great questions at issue, only authority to grant pardons. The Americans contended that there could be no pardon where there was no guilt.

In any event, the Americans were thankful for every day that the British delayed in making their attack. To oppose the enemy's 32,000 men, Washington could assemble only about 20,000 fit for duty, but most of these were recruits or militia hastily summoned for the occasion. There were a few units of the Continental Army present, but none of these had as yet received as much as one year's training.

The defense of New York City was a peculiarly difficult problem. The places to be defended were large islands, and the British fleet had complete control of the sea and the rivers. To try to block passage up the Hudson, two forts were constructed on opposite sides of the river: Fort Washington on the highest point of Manhattan Island and Fort Lee on the Palisades on the New Jersey shore. Sunken ships and other obstacles were placed in the river between the two forts; their guns were sited to cover these obstacles. However, these measures soon proved inadequate when British ships managed to pass the guns of the forts without damage to themselves, proving that the British could sail up the Hudson at any time they wished.

The situation on the eastern side of Manhattan Island was even worse. Here the East River flowed between Manhattan Island and Long Island. If the British could seize Brooklyn Heights on Long Island their artillery would dominate New York City just as effectively as the Americans had dominated Boston from Dorchester Heights. Yet if American forces were sent to defend Long Island, Washington would be splitting his army into two parts separated from each other by a wide stretch of water which the British fleet could control. To divide the army would be to invite destruction in detail. To fail to occupy Brooklyn Heights would ensure the eventual loss of New

York City, yet to do so would be dangerous in the extreme.

From a strictly military point of view the city should have been considered indefensible and abandoned in favor of a position farther upriver. But its loss without a struggle would be a blow to the morale of the colonists, and furthermore Congress wanted it defended. General Washington therefore split his army in two: one part on Long Island under the command of Nathanael Greene who had been appointed to the rank of major general early in August; the remainder under his own direct supervision on Manhattan Island.

During the battles around New York, Washington made several mistakes. This decision to split his forces, part on Long Island and part on Manhattan, was the first. Before long, many army officers would be asking themselves if Washington was the right man to be commander in chief, and wondering if perhaps General Charles Lee, the professional British officer, should be given the job.

It is not surprising that Washington made mistakes, since he had not been trained as a soldier. It is only surprising that he did not make more. That he was capable of learning rapidly would be demonstrated before the year was out, and in two years Lee would prove to everyone's satisfaction that he was not the man.

The Battle of Long Island or Brooklyn Heights: On August 22 the British landed about 15,000 men on Long Island south of the American position. Three days later they brought over about 5,000 more. A large portion of the 20,000 were Hessians. To oppose them the Americans had initially about 4,000 men, but Washington soon sent reinforcements across the East River until the defending Americans totalled about 7,000. At this time General Greene was absent because of sickness. Major General John Sullivan was assigned to command; then four days later Major General Putnam. Washington also arrived on the scene before the battle started. All of this created a certain amount of confusion as to who was responsible, but it appears that Washington intended Putnam to be commander of the troops on Long Island.

General Israel Putnam was a courageous officer from Connecticut who had seen service on the frontier in the French and Indian War and was known throughout New England for a number of sensational exploits. He was a brave, bluff outspoken man, in peacetime a successful farmer and in wartime a popular hero among the New England troops who thought he was a great general and felt he was one of them. In later years he would be remembered by many people, not as the commander at this battle, but as the man who galloped his horse down a flight of rocky steps to escape capture at the hands of British cavalry who were thrilled by this daring feat but dared not duplicate it.

North and east of where the British had landed was a line of hills and woods stretching from Gowanus Bay (through what is now Greenwood Cemetery) through Prospect Park to the east. Three main roads led northward through gaps in the hills, one near the coast and two farther inland. The Americans guarded these three roads with about 2,800 men. There was also a fourth road much farther to the east, but only a small picket was placed there. Most of the remainder of the troops occupied the inner defense line along Brooklyn Heights. It stretched from the shores of Wallabout Bay southeast to a swamp behind what is now the Gowanus Canal. The center of the position was Fort Putnam, the name of which was changed to Fort Greene during the War of 1812. (Located in the center of Fort Greene Park is the Martyrs' Tomb and a monument 145 feet high erected to commemorate the American Seamen, Soldiers and Citizens who perished on the rotting hulks of British prison ships at the Wallabout during the Revolution. The tomb contains the remains of 11,000 patriots.)

Although Washington had rushed reinforcements across

the East River to Long Island, General Howe was in no hurry at all. He had no intention of making a frontal attack up any one of those three roads if he could avoid it. He soon learned of the existence of the fourth road to the east and decided to use it to make a turning movement around the unguarded American left flank. On the night of August 26–27, leaving strong detachments under Generals James Grant and Philip von Heister to make active demonstrations at the three passes in the hills, he marched the main body, 10,000 strong, off to the east. The picket on the fourth road was surprised and overwhelmed. As a result, on the morning of August 27 the enveloping column was well in the rear of the Americans, had turned back to the west, and was marching rapidly to cut off any possible retreat.

Meanwhile General Grant had begun his demonstration up the coastal road. Putnam hastily sent word to Brigadier General William A. "Lord" Stirling, an American officer who claimed he was the rightful heir to a title in Scotland, to reinforce that flank with the nearest troops. Fortunately these included Colonel John Haslet's Delaware, and Colonel William Smallwood's Maryland Continental regiments. Oddly enough, both regiments were temporarily commanded by their majors, the senior officers being absent in New York City serving on courts-martial.

As the battle then developed, Stirling faced Grant on the coastal road and Sullivan faced von Heister on the next two inland roads. At each point the British far outnumbered the Americans, but in accordance with the general plan, made no large-scale attack.

Suddenly at nine o'clock in the morning two heavy signal guns sounded in the rear of Sullivan's position. Simultaneously the troops in their front advanced. Attempting to retreat, the Americans found themselves attacked from the rear. Almost surrounded, they put up a brief but spirited resistance. Sullivan was captured. Some of his men escaped, but most of them were killed, captured or cut down while attempting to surrender. How many were thus cut down is difficult to say, but it was here that the Hessians were for the first but not the last time accused of murdering defenseless men.

General Grant began his advance. He had received reinforcements including 2,000 marines, and outnumbered Stirling by over six to one. Cut off from his line of retreat by Howe's attack to his rear, Stirling had but one hope of saving his command and it was a slim one. To the west on their right flank was the swamp where the Gowanus Canal is now. Stirling acted promptly with resolution and courage. He detailed Major Mordecai Gist with 250 of his Marylanders to counterattack back up the road while the remainder of the troops were ordered to retreat across the swamp. Led by Major Gist and by General Stirling himself, the 250 attacked against overwhelming numbers, were thrown back and attacked again, only to recoil. A total of six times they advanced. As he watched helplessly from Brooklyn Heights where he had come at the sound of the firing, Washington exclaimed, "Good God! What brave fellows I must this day lose!"

Stirling was captured after a stubborn but hopeless fight. Almost all of the 250 were either killed, wounded or taken prisoners. Only 9 men, led by Major Gist, escaped to the American lines, but the counterattack had saved the rest of the Maryland regiment and the Delaware regiment which had retreated through the swamp in good order under a hail of cannonfire and musketry. The Maryland monument near the center of Prospect Park commemorates the entire regiment and their gallant battle. It is inscribed with Washington's heartfelt tribute and IN HONOR OF MARYLAND'S FOUR HUNDRED WHO ON THIS BATTLEFIELD AUGUST 27, 1776, SAVED THE AMERICAN ARMY.

Flushed with success, the British advanced to seize Brooklyn Heights while their enemy was still disorganized; complete victory seemed certain but they were halted at

THE BATTLES AROUND
★ NEW YORK ★

THE BATTLE OF HARLEM HEIGHTS
← British Advance, Sept 16, 1776
← American Attacks, Sept 16, 1776

Fort Tryon
Fort Washington
Fort Lee

Jumel Mansion

Harlem R.
Broadway
Bronx R.
1
1A

Grant's Tomb
St. Nicholas Ave.
25th St.
Bloomingdale Rd.
Central Park
Boston Post Rd.

Hackensack R.
NJ Turnpike
1
9

Hudson River

Pulaski Skyway

57th St.
42nd St.
34th St.

Newtown Creek

Scale of Miles
0 ½ 1 1½

N

KIP'S BAY, SEPT 15
← Putnam's Line of Retreat
← British Advances
••• Roads on Manhattan, 1776
━ Modern Roads Coinciding
-- Tunnels

NJ Turnpike Ext.

Battery Park

Broadway
Manhattan
East R.

27

NEW JERSEY
NEW YORK

27A

Gowanus Bay

PUTNAM

Fort Greene Park

Howe's Line
of March

STIRLING
Greenwood
Cem.
Prospect
Pk.

SULLIVAN
VON HEISTER

27

Staten
Island

J. Downey

GRANT

27A

THE BATTLE OF LONG ISLAND
ΛΛΛ American Outer Defenses
▲▲▲ American Inner Defense Line
← British Attacks, Aug 27, 1776
← Stirling's Counterattacks, Aug 27

the last moment. Knowing that his enemy could not escape, Howe had decided to wait until he could study the situation and make a coordinated attack or conduct a siege at his leisure. He let two days slip by while Washington strengthened his entrenchments and brought more men across the river until 9,000 men stood there with the sea behind them, facing a triumphant enemy of over 22,000.

Washington finally recognized his peril and made his plans to escape. In this emergency he turned for help to Colonel Glover's and Colonel Hutchinson's regiments of Massachusetts fishermen and sailors from Marblehead and Salem. On the night of the 29th, under cover of a thick mist, these men, using every kind of craft they could lay their hands on, silently and efficiently began the evacuation. It was a tremendous task that had been set them —to ferry the army across a wide river of strong, conflicting tides and currents in just one night. Washington himself supervised the embarkation; like the captain of a ship he was in the last boat to leave. When the unsuspecting British awoke at daybreak they were amazed to discover only a deserted line of entrenchments. It did not seem possible but Washington and the fishermen from Massachusetts had saved everything that was left of the entire force.

In this Battle of Long Island the Americans had lost about 1,300 killed, wounded and captured out of 3,800 engaged, while the British and Hessian army of 22,000 engaged had less than 400 casualties. General Howe had proved his ability as a tactician by successfully planning and executing a night march and a wide envelopment of the American position which caught them completely by surprise. It would have helped if the Americans had possessed some cavalry to post on their eastern flank, but cavalry was generally conspicious by its absence in the first years of the war in the north. Taking advantage of the British failure to press their victory and the failure of the British fleet to interpose, Washington had saved the remainder of the force but the morale of his army had suffered. The men naturally thought more about the defeat than they did of the near miracle which had saved them from capture. Thus, as a result of the battle, the Americans on Manhattan faced the prospect of defending New York City with something less than their former high spirits and with fewer effective troops.

The victory was hailed with delight by the Tories in England; General Howe was knighted by the King. In America the people were gloomy and dismayed; the militia around New York departed for home in droves. Washington's army lost far more by desertion than it had in battle.

The Battle of Harlem Heights: The defenders of New York City had been working for several weeks to strengthen and enlarge their fortifications. The old Battery, a line of cannon which crossed the north edge of Battery Park and then ran to the southeast, was strengthened. In 1776 this area was near the water's edge and therefore the Battery protected the city from direct assault from the south or west. The area now called Battery Park was under water then but has since been filled in. Many similar changes have been made all around Manhattan Island so that several of the former small bays and inlets have disappeared.

Using the Battery as the starting point, the defenders extended their fortifications up the island on both sides facing the Hudson River and also the East River. They knew they were open to attack from either side. The British had already proved that their fleet could sail past the forts on the Hudson, and there was nothing to stop them from landing any place they wanted to on the East River shore. But in attempting to be ready everywhere at once, the defenders could not help but spread themselves too thinly.

General Washington recognized the difficulty of his position and asked for the opinions of several people.

Many of them, including General Greene and John Jay, who owned a great deal of property in the city, not only recommended the evacuation of the city but also that it be burned so that the enemy could not use it for winter quarters.

Congress would not permit the city to be burned but finally left it to Washington's discretion as to whether or not it should be evacuated. Preparations were immediately made to leave the city but the decision had come too late. For on September 15, following a heavy naval bombardment, British troops landed at Kip's Bay on the eastern shore near what is now 34th Street. (This is another place where the shore line has been changed. The bay has been filled in to such an extent that the actual landing place is not at the water's edge but inland about 300 yards.)

The small militia force opposite the landing place, paralyzed by the naval bombardment, broke and ran. Even the appearance of General Washington himself could not stay the rout. By virtue of his commanding presence and dominant personality he managed to halt a few, but when about seventy enemy soldiers appeared, these turned again to flee. The commander in chief, who knew he had a violent temper and tried at all times to keep it under control, became so enraged that he lashed out at the fleeing militia with the flat of his sword, but to no avail. For once, discouraged beyond measure, he slumped forward in the saddle and finally permitted one of his staff officers to lead him away when the enemy was only a hundred yards distant.

The American situation was extremely precarious. There was only one main road, the Boston Post Road, which ran the length of Manhattan Island. The British troops advanced immediately from the landing beach, seized and blocked this road, cutting off the normal escape route of the Americans.

General Putnam, who had some 3,000 men in the city,

learned from one of his aides, Major Aaron Burr, that there was a possible alternate route. This was the Bloomingdale Road which branched off the Boston Post Road and, following the general course of Broadway today, stopped short of the present location of Grant's Tomb. From there on the troops would have to go on foot. All the artillery in the city, over seventy guns—about half of the artillery in the army—would therefore have to be abandoned. This would make for faster marching, and time was of the essence for there was no reason to believe that the British would not make a swift drive across the island and cut the defending forces in half.

Hurrying his men out of the city across footlanes and farmpaths, Putnam struck the Bloomingdale Road at about 59th Street (the southwest corner of Central Park) and pushed them onward as fast as possible. Encouraging, exhorting and driving troops forward was just the sort of work Putnam could do best.

It was a long line of soldiers that moved out of New York on that day. It could have been broken very easily at any point if the British had chosen to do so, but they were making no move in that direction. Their first division of 4,000 men had secured the beachhead and blocked the Boston Post Road, thus accomplishing the assigned mission. In accordance with the announced plan, they were waiting for the second division of 9,000 men to land before making any further advance.

General Howe had been accused of being too cautious, but of course he had no way of knowing that the defenders would break and run so fast; he had expected more opposition. There is also the delightful tale of Mrs. Robert Murray who invited General Howe and his officers to tea and so diverted them that they forgot to supervise the movements of their troops for a couple of hours, thus delaying the British advance across the island and giving Putnam and his men their chance to escape. Since Howe knew that his troops were moving exactly according to plan, he probably saw no harm in relaxing for a while, so Mrs. Murray did not alter the scheme of maneuver in any way, but if Howe had not gone to tea he might have seen his opportunity to speed his men forward.

When the British began their advance up the Boston Post Road we find the unusual condition of two columns of troops marching north in parallel columns separated by little more than the width of Central Park, each completely unaware of the existence of the other. When they did finally come together it was entirely by accident. As the British advance guard on the Post Road reached the point where it entered the east side of present-day Central Park, it encountered Colonel William Smallwood and the remainder of the Maryland regiment which had fought so gallantly on Long Island. These troops turned the British into the road leading across Central Park where they met the rear guard of Putnam's column. There was a sharp skirmish which lasted only a short time until the Americans retreated north—Putnam had escaped.

That night Washington gathered about 10,000 men together to defend Harlem Heights, a rocky plateau stretching across Manhattan Island from the Hudson to the Harlem River. Just south of Harlem Heights is a long, wide ravine known in colonial days as the Hollow Way (today the western half of 125th Street generally follows this ravine between Harlem Heights on the north and the high ground on which Grant's Tomb was built on the south). On the morning of September 16 the colonial troops were posted in lines on the heights north of the Hollow Way awaiting attack.

From his headquarters in the historic Jumel Mansion (which still stands just one block east of St. Nicholas Avenue which here corresponds to the route of the Boston Post Road), Washington took stock of the situation. His troops were for the most part tired and discouraged. He had lost over 350 men plus the city of

New York and half of the army's artillery and had inflicted hardly any damage on the enemy. In addition to the loss of Long Island, this was almost too much; even Washington had begun to lose confidence in the ability of his men to fight. Somehow he had to win a victory, even a small one, to prove that the British were not invincible.

Early on the morning of September 16, Lieutenant Colonel Thomas Knowlton, who had done so well at Bunker Hill, led a reconnaissance party of 120 Rangers, all volunteers, forward across the Hollow Way. By daybreak they had advanced to a point below Broadway and what is now 110th Street (which forms the north edge of Central Park) where they were spotted by the British pickets. A brief skirmish ensued before Knowlton retreated, pursued by superior numbers. As the men recrossed the Hollow Way a bugler in the British Light Infantry stood up on the high ground (just north of where Grant's Tomb is now) and sounded the hunting call that the fox had gone to ground. The implication was only too clear—Washington, the old gray fox, and his army were caught at last.

The insult could not have been lost on that old foxhunter George Washington, but in spite of the anger he must have felt he saw his opportunity. He sent a small force into the Hollow Way to lure the enemy forward. The British infantry advanced, driving the decoy force up north toward the heights. Then Washington sent a selected detachment composed of Knowlton's Rangers, most of whom were from Connecticut, and Virginia troops led by Major Andrew Leitch, to make a left hook behind the advancing British and cut them off. Premature firing of a musket disclosed the flank attack. The British immediately realized their danger and started falling back. Both Knowlton and Leitch fell mortally wounded in the attack, but even with their leaders gone, the men pressed forward.

Seeing that the enemy were on the run, Washington reinforced the attack and made sure to include the militia who had run from Kip's Bay so that they might redeem themselves. The British retired south into a buckwheat field where they received reinforcements and made a stand. The British held their ground here for about two hours until their ammunition began to run low when they again started to retreat.

At this point Washington ordered his troops to withdraw; he had no desire to bring on a general engagement. It was just as well, since large numbers of British reinforcements were nearing the scene. Some Americans did not receive the orders right away and pursued as far as 110th Street before breaking off the action.

Out of some 2,000 men engaged, this battle cost the Americans less than 130 casualties. The British, who probably had about the same number engaged, reported various casualty figures; 200 killed, wounded and missing is a fairly accurate estimate. This was therefore only a small engagement, but it was a tremendous boost to American morale. For the first time they had won a victory in open warfare. They had stood their ground, then made a successful counterattack, and had kept driving forward, retreating only when ordered to do so. Furthermore, troops from the various colonies had worked together in harmony and acquired respect for each other. No additional attacks were made on the American lines, and nearly a month passed before General Howe made any further advance.

VII

From the Loss of New York City to Trenton and Princeton

IN the summer and early fall of 1776, while the British and American armies were fighting for possession of New York City and the lower Hudson Valley, other forces were striving for control of Lake Champlain in upper New York.

When the Americans retreated from Canada they were in wretched condition. Most, if not all of them, should have been in a hospital but there were no such facilities. The local commanders did what they could but it was difficult to fight disease without proper medical aid. Congress sent Major General Horatio Gates north to take command, which for a time did nothing but confuse the issue, since General Philip Schuyler was still in command of the New York Department. They finally settled the problem between themselves by Schuyler's assuming the role of what we would call today a theater commander while Gates became the commander of the troops. Together they did the best they could to remedy the situation by obtaining better food and some decent clothing. At one point they had only about 1,000 men but they called on the militia, were sent a few Continental regiments as reinforcements, and eventually could count over 10,000 men, with about 6,500 fit for duty.

This was a great improvement but it was not nearly enough. By early September, General Guy Carleton had an army of 13,000 men, of whom 5,000 were German mercenaries. However, both sides knew that no large invading force could possibly advance rapidly through the almost trackless forests; control of Lake Champlain would be vital to the success of an army moving southward. Therefore, throughout the summer and early fall the Americans and the British bent every effort to construct a fleet of ships capable of sailing and fighting on the lake.

Because of his experience as a shipper and merchant before the war, Benedict Arnold was charged with construction and command of the fleet. He had three schooners and a sloop to start with, but all kinds of auxiliary craft were needed. The only wood available was in the form of standing trees, but there were three neglected old sawmills in the area. Yet there were no tools, ropes, canvas, anchors or any other of the supplies so necessary to the building of naval vessels. Arnold set to work with his usual indomitable energy, imported ship carpenters and sailmakers and set the soldiers to work felling trees. Sceptics believed that the whole effort was a waste of time. But the ships were not only built—they were also manned, and the men trained to sail them and fire their guns.

General Carleton had quite a different problem. There were ships on the St. Lawrence but they could not pass the rapids on the Richelieu River. His ships were therefore dismantled, carried up in pieces, and completely rebuilt at St. Johns. In one way or another the auxiliary vessels were constructed or similarly transported overland or dragged through the rapids. Both sides showed unusual ingenuity and resourcefulness in this contest. By early

October the little fleets were ready, although Carleton's was much stronger in fire power than Arnold's.

The Battle of Valcour Island began on October 11. It lasted for two days, and when this first engagement between a British and an American fleet was over, Arnold's little navy had been destroyed. Lake Champlain was entirely under British control, but the season was so far advanced that Carleton decided to retreat into Canada. Arnold had lost the battle, but by building a fleet and forcing the British to build a larger one in order to win control of the lake, he had gained so much time that the invasion of upper New York was delayed until the following year. It has been said with some justification that Arnold's delaying action at Lake Champlain may have saved the Revolution. If Carleton had been able to take Fort Ticonderoga and use it as a base of supplies to support an advance the following year, Burgoyne's expedition, starting from there, might not have ended at Saratoga.

While the opposing forces on Lake Champlain were proving themselves so adept at shipbuilding and naval warfare, the armies on Manhattan Island, following the Battle of Harlem Heights on September 16, prepared for the next encounter. Five days after the battle a large fire broke out in New York City, destroying most of the downtown section. Knowing that several general officers had at one time or another advised Washington to burn the city when he retreated, the British accused the Americans of having started the fire. This accusation was never proven. It was undoubtedly accidental, but at the same time it temporarily impaired the city's value as a base of operations and made the problems of occupation more difficult.

Earlier on the same day of the fire, Captain Nathan Hale of Connecticut, one of Colonel Knowlton's Rangers, was captured on Long Island in the disguise of a Dutch schoolteacher. The following day he was hanged as a spy, but the famous statement which tradition credits to him, "I only regret that I have but one life to lose for my country," remained as a source of inspiration to his fellow men. And inspiration was to be needed soon, for within the next two months came a period of dark despair when the American Revolution seemed sure to fail.

On October 12, the second day of the Battle of Valcour Island, the British sailed up the East River and landed in lower New York on a peninsula projecting out from the mainland. When they tried to advance, Colonel Edward Hand and his Pennsylvania rifle regiment stopped them along a narrow causeway. Whereupon General Howe waited six days before making another landing, a few more miles to the northeast. Here his troops were met by Colonel John Glover's Massachusetts brigade which engaged them in a brisk fire fight and delayed their advance. Four days later there occurred the first instance of Americans fighting in large organized units against each other. Colonel John Haslet's Delaware Continentals made a night attack on the Queen's American Rangers led by Major Robert Rogers whose ranger force had become famous during the French and Indian War. This Loyalist regiment fought well during the Revolution but Major Rogers soon resigned.

On October 18, the same day that Howe made his second landing on the mainland of New York, Washington started to withdraw northward from Manhattan Island. Owing to a shortage of horses and wagons, the artillery pieces were pulled by hand; progress was very slow and there was every reason to believe that the British would soon be standing in the way to end the retreat. Fortunately for the American cause, General Howe was again moving slowly. Days passed while additional troops, artillery and supplies of all kinds were brought ashore. In the end the story of the retreats from Brooklyn Heights and Kip's Bay was repeated; the Americans escaped to White Plains where Washington took up a defensive position. The British simply followed. The battle fought on October 28 did not involve the whole of either army. One American brigade, commanded by General Alexander McDougall, occupying an isolated position on a hill on the right flank, was attacked and forced backward off the hill to join the main body. A few days later Washington moved to a strong position a few miles in the rear to await another attack which did not come.

Realizing the futility of chasing his enemy in the same fashion still farther to the north, General Howe turned back to take advantage of one of the biggest mistakes of the war. When Washington had retreated from Manhattan he had left large garrisons behind in Fort Washington and also in Fort Lee across the Hudson on the New Jersey shore. Throughout the war the Continental Congress continued to advise commanders in the field, not only in matters of general policy which was entirely proper and appropriate, but also in the actual handling of strictly military problems that could only be decided by the officer in command on the spot. In addition, Congress had directed Washington to consult with his generals upon matters of major military importance. In his modesty the commander in chief in the early years of the war seems to have construed this directive too literally. The decision to retain garrisons at Forts Washington and Lee is an excellent example of how the Congress, and too great a consideration for his generals' opinions, led Washington into grave errors. Congress wanted the forts held if practicable, and the majority of generals, including, most unfortunately, General Greene who was in command, believed it could be done. Washington did not agree but gave Greene discretionary orders as to withdrawal.

On November 16 Lieutenant General Wilhelm von Knyphausen, who had been assigned by Howe to capture Fort Washington, launched his soldiers in a well-planned, co-ordinated assault upon the fort. The attacking troops

battle fought on October 28, did not involve the whole
of either army. One American brigade, commanded by
General Alexander McDougall, received the greater

FROM THE LOSS
OF NEW YORK CITY
☆ TO TRENTON ☆
AND PRINCETON

SCALE OF MILES
0   100   200

exhibited great bravery in storming the walls and were met by defenders of equal stubbornness, but the result was a foregone conclusion. Over 2,600 prisoners were captured plus all the guns of the fort and its redoubts—a tremendous loss to Washington's army.

Fort Washington itself has not been preserved, but the site of one of the more important redoubts has been. It was strengthened and enlarged by the British and named Fort Tryon in honor of the royal governor of New York. Today, from the high point in Fort Tryon Park where the redoubt was located, there is a magnificent view up the Hudson. It was in defense of this redoubt on November 16, 1776 that Margaret Corbin, carrying water to the men serving the guns, saw her husband fall severely wounded. She bravely took his place and helped keep the gun in action. Her heroism is not only commemorated at Fort Tryon but also on a plaque on the wall of the cemetery at West Point. She is the only person honored in this way at the military academy.

Meanwhile Washington had crossed the Hudson farther up the river with a portion of his command. General Charles Lee, who had returned from Charleston, and General William Heath were left in New York to guard against the possibility of another British advance to the north. On the night of November 19–20 Cornwallis moved against Fort Lee. The garrison escaped but more guns and ammunition were lost in their hasty withdrawal.

The Americans were now in a most unenviable position. With the loss of 2,600 men at Fort Washington they could do nothing but remain on the defensive and wait for the British to advance. The army was divided into two parts; Generals Lee and Heath were guarding New York, while Washington was watching New Jersey with that portion of the army which had come with him across the Hudson plus those who had escaped from Fort Lee. The initiative was entirely in the hands of General Howe whose attention now centered on New Jersey. He sent

Cornwallis to pursue Washington with a large force of British and Hessians.

Forced back by superior numbers but giving ground as slowly as possible, fighting delaying actions wherever he could, Washington retreated across New Jersey. One of his first acts was to call upon General Lee to come to his aid. The latter crossed over to New Jersey but moved no farther than Morristown, paying no attention at all to orders sent to him day after day for almost a month. It appeared that General Lee was purposely leaving Washington to his fate. If the commander in chief were to suffer a disastrous defeat the Congress would surely then call upon General Lee, the second in command, to save the people.

Washington's command was rapidly melting away. The militia were deserting in droves. Winter was fast approaching, and on the 31st of the year the enlistment of most of the regulars, the Continentals, would expire. Fortunately at this moment, on the morning of December 13, British dragoons captured Lee having breakfast at an inn in the town of Basking Ridge, New Jersey, twelve miles southwest of Morristown. Whether or not Lee recognized any of his captors, he surely recognized their uniforms, because when he had been in the British army he had served with that same regiment.

The dragoons could not possibly have performed a greater service to the Continental cause. Not only had Lee intentionally delayed in coming to help Washington, but he had also been writing letters denouncing him. In fact Lee had just finished a letter to General Gates describing the commander in chief as "damnably deficient" when the dragoons appeared.

Commander Lee's division passed to John Sullivan, who together with General Stirling had been exchanged after the Battle of Brooklyn Heights. Sullivan promptly marched to join Washington. His arrival increased the effective strength from about 3,000 to 5,000 but this was still not enough to fight Cornwallis' greatly superior forces. Washington retreated across the Delaware into Pennsylvania, taking with him to his side of the river every boat for several miles up- and downstream. The Continental Congress voted to leave Philadelphia, then fled in haste to Baltimore.

General Howe concluded that the campaign was at an end. The patriot army had practically dissolved; winter would do the rest. He directed Cornwallis, who agreed with his decision, to leave strong detachments at various selected posts and have them go into winter quarters. The year 1777 would surely see the end of the war and with very little further trouble.

In this same mood of optimism the British also undertook another expedition designed to secure a base of operations for reducing New England. Escorted by the fleet, General Clinton seized Newport, Rhode Island, early in December. When the new year opened and good campaigning weather arrived the British would be ready to crush the revolt.

VIII

The Battle of Trenton

WHEN, after the long retreat through New Jersey, Washington was forced across the Delaware, his army had dwindled to a mere fraction of its former strength and numbered less than 3,000 men. Even after General Sullivan brought Lee's division into camp the number was only increased to a possible 5,000. The arrival of General Gates and of General John Cadwalader with some Pennsylvania volunteers brought the total strength to 6,000 effectives, a pitifully small force indeed to oppose the British Army. Furthermore, in just a few days time the year would end and the army would practically disappear. Like Montgomery and Arnold at Quebec the year before, Washington found himself forced to do something before December 31 or his troops would go home, their enlistments expired. Only about 1,400 men were due to remain with him after that date.

The British had now decided that the campaign was over. From their point of view this was not an unreasonable assumption. The colonial forces had been defeated at every turn, driven sixty miles through New Jersey, and seemed utterly incapable of any offensive action. From all appearances their enemy was so reduced in strength and so demoralized that it was not worth the effort to pursue them. Furthermore they knew that if they just waited a few days most of the colonial soldiers would simply go home at the end of the year. It seemed appropriate to go into winter quarters, which was in any event the normal custom of European armies at that time.

So the British and Hessian troops were disposed in comfortable quarters along an extended line stretching from the Delaware back to New York. Some 3,000 men under Colonel Carl von Donop were posted along the river, half of them based in Trenton (then a small town of about a hundred houses), the other half at Bordentown and Burlington which were respectively 7 and 17 miles downstream to the southeast. Headquarters was established at New Brunswick, 27 miles to the rear. General Howe settled down to spend a comfortable winter in New York while Cornwallis made preparations to return to England.

Thus the British presented the opportunity of having their detachments attacked individually, but few leaders would even have considered the possibility. Most men would have been fully occupied simply trying to keep themselves and their troops alive. Yet even before Sullivan's arrival Washington had begun to consider what might be done.

The plan that he decided upon was a desperate one because it involved not just the risk of a battle from which he might retreat, but the loss of his army in case of failure. He intended to cross the Delaware with his entire force and strike at Trenton and Burlington; if defeated, the river would be at his back, destruction almost certain.

Three columns were to cross: one above Trenton, a smaller one just below the town, and a third below Burlington. Washington was to command the main force of about 2,500 crossing above Trenton and attacking the town from the north. The second, smaller unit, consisting of some 700 men, under Brigadier General James Ewing, was to take up a position south of Assunpink Creek and prevent the enemy's escape in that direction. Cadwalader was to command the third unit of about 2,000 troops. His mission was to land near Burlington and engage the enemy, defeating him if possible, but at least keeping him occupied and unable to move to the defense of Trenton, and creating as great a diversion as possible.

The less said about the second and third columns the better. Ewing took one look at the river and made no effort to carry out his mission. About 600 of Cadwalader's men made their way to the New Jersey shore but were then told to return because their two fieldpieces could not be landed safely.

The troops in Washington's column began marching toward the river in midafternoon of Christmas Day. It was bitterly cold, the wind was rising, and the ill-clad men felt it keenly. Yet without hesitation, under the spur of Washington's determined leadership, they began their embarkation at dark, Brigadier General Adam Stephen's Virginia Continentals loading first. The river was full of floating ice, making the crossing most dangerous at night, but again the army found itself in the care of Colonel John Glover's amphibious regiment which had saved them at Long Island. About an hour before midnight, hail and sleet began to fall, driven in gusts by the wind. The passage was delayed but Glover's men got them safely across and before dawn they were able to begin the march to Trenton. Even for men fully clad with proper boots the march would have been severe, but many started in bare feet over the snow, and made it. The difference between what this column was to accomplish that day and the failure of the other two is truly striking. The endurance and fortitude of the American soldier when resolutely and capably led has been demonstrated on many occasions throughout history but never more forcibly.

Washington's command marched on Trenton in two columns. General Greene took the Pennington Road on the northern flank while General Sullivan took the road near the river. About eight o'clock on the morning of December 26 both columns struck the Hessian pickets on their roads almost simultaneously and drove them into Trenton. The timing between columns was almost perfect, but the whole movement was hours later than originally planned due to the excessive difficulties of crossing in the winter storm. The prime question was how much chance was there of a complete surprise of the garrison. Success depended upon that single factor. If the enemy were ready they could undoubtedly hold out long enough to be reinforced, then Washington and his army might be caught on the wrong side of the river.

All was quiet in Trenton until the moment of the attack. The town was held by 1,400 Hessian troops commanded by Colonel Johann Rall, almost all of whom had spent Christmas Eve and Christmas Day celebrating by feasting and drinking in the hearty German fashion, with no worries about the Americans across the river. On the morning of December 26 they were not exactly well prepared to resist attack although Colonel Rall had received a warning during the night. While he was at a party a man tried to talk to him but the servants refused to let him pass. The visitor then wrote a note to say that the Americans were coming. It was delivered to Rall who shoved it in his pocket and probably never read it. The note was found there after his death two days later.

The Battle of Trenton turned out to be one of the most one-sided affairs ever recorded in history. Washington's plan was executed flawlessly. Greene's troops deployed to the northeast to prevent escape in that direction and guard against possible enemy reinforcement while others of his units, under Brigadier General Hugh Mercer, swung to the right to attack from the northwest. In the center Stirling's brigade seized the north end of Warren and

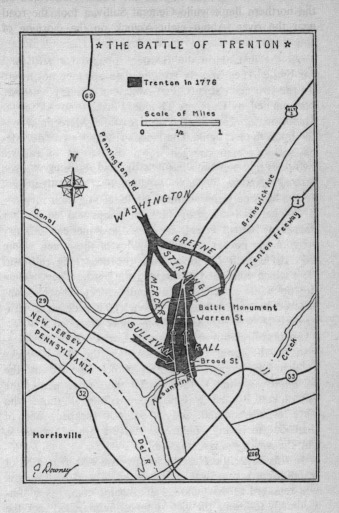

Broad Streets, called King and Queen Streets in Revolutionary times. Here the artillery was placed to sweep these two main streets with fire. (The 150-foot Trenton Battle Monument marks the spot where the guns went into position.)

At the first alarm the Hessians poured forth to form for battle. They bravely attempted to advance northward up the two main streets. The American artillery batteries, commanded by Captains Thomas Forrest and Alexander Hamilton, fired down the streets while Mercer's troops fell upon the left flank. The Hessians withdrew in disorder as Stirling's men charged down the streets to capture two guns that had been hastily emplaced. Here on Warren Street, Captain William Washington and Lieutenant James Monroe were wounded while leading their men.

Colonel Rall rallied his Hessian troops and led another charge up Broad Street. By now the American infantry were in the houses along both sides of the street, where they dried their flintlocks from the drenching rain and sleet which continued throughout the battle. They opened fire upon the attackers with deadly effect. The Hessians faltered and fell back. As Colonel Rall ordered a withdrawal, he was struck down, mortally wounded.

Meanwhile Sullivan's troops had driven back the Hessians in the lower part of town near the Old Barracks (which has been restored and is now located on the Statehouse grounds), then seized the bridge across the Assunpink. Retreat was now impossible; all those who were left surrendered. Only about 400 escaped, most of them due to Ewing's failure to arrive south of the creek, but the victory was complete.

In this battle the Hessian troops lost 970 men, 920 of whom were taken away as prisoners. The American loss was reported as 4 wounded, an amazing comparison. Immediately following the victory the army marched back the way it had come through the storm of snow and sleet which continued to rage throughout the night as they recrossed the river. Two men are reported to have frozen to death on the return trip; the only wonder is that there were not more. Some of the men had fought and marched more than thirty miles in the most bitter weather.

Immediately following the victory Colonel von Donop also marched. He evacuated Bordentown and Burlington and withdrew farther into New Jersey.

The effect of the battle upon the people of the country was electric. Washington's reputation as a military leader had been declining rapidly as a result of the series of lost battles and long retreats. Now he was hailed as a genius. The cause which had seemed hopelessly lost was given new life.

IX

The Princeton Campaign

ON December 27, 1776, the day after the Battle of Trenton, General Washington and his men were safely back across the Delaware in Pennsylvania. Then came the surprising news that General Cadwalader, who had failed to cross the river to co-operate in the battle, had now done so and was in New Jersey. This unexpected development split the American forces into two parts. Rather than have Cadwalader return again to the Pennsylvania shore without having accomplished anything, Washington decided to concentrate at Trenton.

By the end of December there were 5,000 men collected together at Trenton but it was not an effective fighting force. The enlistments of most of the Continentals had expired. Many of the best soldiers were on their way home. Some had been persuaded to remain an extra month or six weeks by the promise of a bounty. The remainder of the men were completely inexperienced militia, mostly from Pennsylvania, who had just arrived in camp. If the British acted promptly the entire American army, caught with its back against the Delaware River, could be destroyed.

When the news of the Battle of Trenton reached General Howe he was stunned. He immediately canceled General Cornwallis' home leave and sent that officer to take command in New Jersey. Lord Charles Cornwallis was a far more energetic soldier than Howe; of the senior British generals in the American Revolution he was undoubtedly the most aggressive and the most skillful. Hurrying south from New York City, gathering in the garrisons stationed along the line to augment his strength Cornwallis reached Princeton on the evening of January 1, 1777.

The next morning he marched toward Trenton. The weather, which had made Washington's march to the Battle of Trenton so difficult, now favored the Americans. During the night it had rained heavily, the temperature had risen, and the roads filled with mud; Cornwallis' progress was necessarily slow. He ran into large bodies of American troops commanded by Colonel Edward Hand and General Greene who occupied a series of successive delaying positions. It was not until late in the afternoon that the British advance reached Washington's main line of defense, established south of Assunpink Creek. In the fading twilight of that winter evening a few attempts were made to cross the creek, but when Cornwallis arrived with the main body he decided to wait until daylight the next morning. He was sure that the Americans were in a trap from which there was no escape.

In this crisis Washington called a conference of his senior officers. It was obvious that their chances of successfully defending Assunpink Creek were slim. A defeat would mean the probable loss of most of the army, since there were not sufficient boats on hand below Trenton to cross into Pennsylvania. An attempt to retreat across the Delaware would have the same ruinous effect. Someone mentioned the possibility of moving in the opposite direction, avoiding the British post at Maidenhead (now Lawrenceville), marching toward Princeton, and striking the main supply base at New Brunswick.

Who originally made the suggestion for this surprising

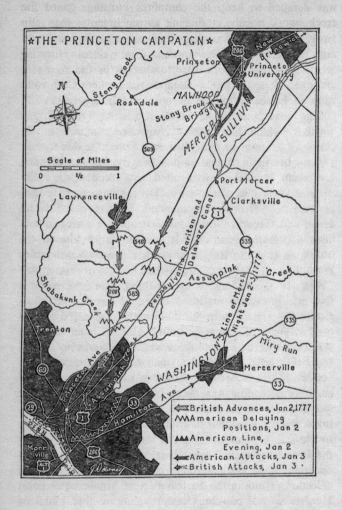

★ THE PRINCETON CAMPAIGN ★

New Brunswick

Princeton
Princeton University

Stony Brook

Rosedale

MAWHOOD

Stony Brook Bridge

MERCER

SULLIVAN

N

Scale of Miles
0   1/2   1

Lawrenceville

Port Mercer

Clarksville

Pennsylvania Raritan and Delaware Canal

Assunpink Creek

Shabakunk Creek

Line of March Night Jan 2-3, 1777

WASHINGTON'S

Trenton

Princeton Ave

Assunpink Creek

Miry Run

Mercerville

Hamilton Ave

Monrisville

PENN.
N.J.

J. Downey

⟨⟨⟨ British Advances, Jan 2, 1777
ʌʌʌ American Delaying
         Positions, Jan 2
▲▲▲ American Line,
         Evening, Jan 2
◀━━ American Attacks, Jan 3
◆◀ British Attacks, Jan 3

move around the enemy flank has never been established but Washington adopted it. A group of some 400 men was detailed to keep the campfires burning, guard the creek, work noisily at digging entrenchments, then slip away at daybreak. The gun wheels were muffled with old rags, and absolute silence was enjoined on everyone as the army moved across Cornwallis' front. Here again the weather favored the American cause. A cold wind from the northwest froze the roads so that the army did not encounter the mud which had slowed the British during the day. This did not mean that the march was easily made because the road was new. All the stumps had not been cleared; in the darkness men continually fell over them and the gun wheels caught frequently.

At daybreak as the army neared Princeton, Brigadier General Mercer was sent to the left to seize the Stony Brook Bridge. His mission was to defend the crossing there to delay pursuit by Cornwallis who could be expected to return to Princeton. The main body under Washington and Sullivan continued toward the town.

Marching along this road toward Trenton was a regiment of British infantry reinforced by some dragoons and a part of another regiment. The remainder of the second regiment was following at about a mile. A third regiment had been left in Princeton to guard the supplies there. The British commander, Lieutenant Colonel Charles Mawhood, had just crossed the bridge when to his amazement he discovered Mercer's force behind him. The surprise was mutual; it was a perfect example of a meeting engagement with neither side expecting to run into the enemy.

Colonel Mawhood immediately faced his men about and double-timed them back over the bridge toward a hill on the east side of the brook. Simultaneously General Mercer recognized the tactical value of this piece of rising ground and raced his men toward it. The two forces met in an orchard at the top where the British executed a bayonet charge and drove the Americans back in confusion. General Mercer, trying to rally his men, was overtaken, bayoneted, and left for dead. Colonel John Haslet, the only member of the Delaware regiment present, was killed. The British pursued, met another small force under General Cadwalader, and routed it also.

At this moment General Washington galloped onto the field of battle. With utter disregard for his personal safety he rode within thirty yards of the British line, calling on the retreating men to come back into the fight. A volley rang out. The smoke completely hid Washington from view, but when it cleared that tall, impressive figure on the great white horse was still there encouraging his men to go forward. At this moment some Continental troops from Sullivan's column arrived, formed a line, and advanced. Heavily outnumbered now, Colonel Mawhood abandoned his guns, ordered a charge and personally led it straight through the American ranks, then turned about and gained the road to Trenton. The whole action had taken just fifteen minutes. Washington personally conducted a vigorous pursuit in which several prisoners were captured. (The site of this, the main engagement of the Battle of Princeton, is now a state park. The Thomas Clarke farmhouse where General Mercer died of his wounds still stands near the southeast end of the park. The Revolutionary burial ground is located near the northern end where the action began. It is a memorial to British and American soldiers who died there.)

While the main battle was being fought in this area a secondary engagement occurred farther to the north. General Sullivan defeated the remainder of the British force and drove it into Princeton where some took refuge in Nassau Hall of the College of New Jersey (as the University was called until it became Princeton). Soon after Captain Alexander Hamilton's battery began firing on Nassau Hall the British surrendered.

Washington had hoped to push on to the main British

supply base at New Brunswick but there was a limit to human endurance. His men had been under arms for forty hours in bitterly cold weather with practically no food. He could not risk a pitched battle with Cornwallis' fresh troops who were surely already marching back from Trenton. Washington therefore moved toward Morristown where his army could go into winter quarters yet still be in a position on Howe's flank to threaten any move the British might make through New Jersey or up the Hudson.

Washington was correct in assuming that his enemy was already on the march. Cornwallis was moving with great speed, urging his men forward. When he reached the site of Stony Brook Bridge, which the Americans had destroyed to slow his advance, he lost no time, but drove his soldiers on through the icy waters to Princeton. So rapidly had the British marched that they entered the town at the same time that the American rearguard marched out. Cornwallis then kept on to New Brunswick to protect that base rather than continue in direct pursuit.

The casualties at the Battle of Princeton have never been accurately determined. As usual the reports on both sides are conflicting. The Americans probably had about 100 killed and wounded. The British losses must have been about the same, but in addition Washington reported nearly 300 prisoners taken.

The two small but decisive Battles of Trenton and Princeton had saved the American army and temporarily saved Philadelphia, the capital of the colonies. It is said that after studying the campaign, Frederick the Great, classified it as one of the most brilliant in military history.

X

From Trenton and Princeton to Saratoga

FOR the moment the tide had turned. When the people of New Jersey heard of the victories at Trenton and Princeton they rose to act in their own defense. Individually and in small groups they attacked and surprised outposts, wagon trains and foraging parties. The enemy detachments scattered throughout the colony were hastily withdrawn and concentrated in the general vicinity of New York. Even their return marches were not accomplished without considerable difficulty and harassment at the hands of the patriots.

Thus most of New Jersey was rescued from the control of the British, yet the army which had made it all possible was in dire straits. The Continental soldiers who had agreed to stay a month or six weeks beyond the expiration of their enlistments were now returning to their homes. At Morristown, Washington was forced to rely upon very temporary reinforcements of militia in order to keep up appearances. At times it seemed as if the army would completely disintegrate. Somehow Washington kept its spirit alive, and after months of strenuous effort formed a new army. Although most of the men were recruits, many had seen service in earlier campaigns and a number of them were finally enlisted for a period of three years.

One of the most difficult problems encountered by Washington in organizing the army was the question of rank for the officers. Each colony wanted its share of officers, regardless of ability. Congressmen pushed forward their favorites. As if these problems were not sufficient to occupy Washington's attention, a steadily increasing flow of foreign adventurers began to arrive. Most of these had been promised high rank by American agents abroad. The only way that Washington could possibly provide commands for them would be to supersede competent American officers, and this he refused to do. He insisted that the Revolution must be fought by an American army commanded by American officers, and that to win the war he had to rely upon those he knew to be capable of command. One of the most important requirements for a leader is the ability to select good subordinates. Many officers whom Congress forced upon Washington proved incompetent but it was rare indeed when an officer whom he himself selected failed in his duty. Outstanding among the foreign officers he selected for high command during the war were the Marquis de Lafayette, the Polish patriots Thaddeus Kosciusko and Casimir Pulaski, and the German Johann de Kalb and Friedrich Wilhelm von Steuben.

It was not until the end of May that Washington felt his new force was sufficiently ready to take the field. He then marched close to New Brunswick, New Jersey. This was not intended as an offensive move but rather as an attempt to discover the British plans for the summer campaign which would surely begin soon. During the preceding winter he had received reports that a large army was being sent to Canada to invade the colonies. He had written to New England and to New York urging that the militia be readied to repel an invasion. Now, by maintaining close contact with General Howe's troops, he hoped to determine what part the British forces in New

Jersey and in New York were to play in the invasion plan.

The British objective was in fact exactly what could have been expected, a repetition of the previous year's attempt to separate New England from the rest of the colonies. The plan, prepared in London, was to have a large force invade New York from Canada via Lake Champlain, then march southward to meet the British advancing northward from New York City up the Hudson River.

The invading force from Canada was to be commanded by Lieutenant General John Burgoyne, and this time it was to start much sooner than General Carleton's effort of the previous year. The British had no intention of being caught again only part way and then being forced to return to Canada when winter came. Burgoyne began his march in June, 1777.

In this same month General Howe, instead of preparing to move northward to meet Burgoyne, undertook a series of small offensive operations in New Jersey. From Washington's point of view these could be merely feints to try to conceal Howe's true objective which certainly should be a march up the Hudson. On the other hand, they could be an effort to find out how much opposition would be encountered if Philadelphia were the target and the British troops were to march overland. Washington had already realized that General Howe might decide to take Philadelphia and had warned Congress of the possibility. Yet it did not make good sense to believe that Howe would do this when the only really logical move would be to go due north.

General Howe evacuated New Jersey and withdrew to New York City and Staten Island where he began active preparations for an expedition of some sort. On July 23 the British fleet sailed southward with a force numbering between 15,000 and 18,000 men. Their destination was assumed to be some point near Philadelphia but Washington could not be certain. At this point the British had all the freedom to maneuver which only control of the sea could afford them. They could move toward Philadelphia, and if Washington followed too far toward the capital, turn and sail back to the Hudson, arriving long before the marching troops could return to protect New York. The smaller American force which had been left near West Point could not possibly stop the advance of General Howe's entire army.

As a temporary measure Washington moved part way to the Delaware River, holding his army in readiness for a march in either direction. On July 30 the British fleet was sighted off the Capes of the Delaware, so Washington moved to Germantown (then a separate town north of Philadelphia and not a part of the city as it is now). Then the fleet disappeared again. If Howe were to turn back to New York, Washington's army was now out of position. Messengers were hastily dispatched to warn the troops near West Point of the possibility of Howe's return. Washington made preparations for retracing his steps, but the fleet reappeared south of the Capes and after a few more days sailed up the Chesapeake. At last Washington could be sure that Philadelphia was the objective.

That General Howe's moves were puzzling to Washington is not surprising, because they have puzzled historians ever since. There is no doubt that the planners in London expected Howe to meet Burgoyne. Explicit orders for him to co-operate were prepared for Lord George Germain, the colonial secretary, but through carelessness on his part were never dispatched. At a later date Germain approved Howe's Philadelphia expedition but expressed a hope that it would be completed in time for him to march up the Hudson.

Whether he received explicit orders or not, the safety of Burgoyne's army should have weighed more heavily upon General Howe's mind than the capture of a city,

FROM TRENTON
☆ AND PRINCETON ☆
TO SARATOGA

Quebec

MAINE

Montreal

Lake
Champlain   VERMONT

NEW
HAMPSHIRE

Lake Ontario
Oswego   Saratoga   Bennington   MASSACHUSETTS

Oriskany   Mohawk
Albany

NEW YORK   Kingston   CONN.   R.I.

West Point

Forts Clinton and Montgomery
Morristown
PENNSYLVANIA   New Brunswick   New York
Princeton

Trenton
Germantown
Brandywine   Philadelphia
NEW JERSEY

MARYLAND   DELAWARE

W. VA.   SCALE OF MILES
0   100   200

VIRGINIA
Chesapeake
Bay

J. Downey

even though that city was the capital of the colonies. Over the years many historians have advanced various theories as to why Howe chose to go to Philadelphia. Among other things he has been accused of trying to grab the spotlight for himself by seizing the capital, thus relegating Burgoyne to a minor role in the eyes of the public. This explanation seems unjust and out of keeping with Howe's previous record. He had proved himself to be a loyal subordinate on many occasions in the French and Indian War in America and in European wars.

A better explanation of General Howe's motives would be that he entirely underestimated the amount of resistance that Burgoyne would meet in his advance from Canada. No British officer in that day and age could visualize the possibility of a British army being forced to surrender to the American rebels. Burgoyne might meet some difficulties along the way but surely nothing he could not overcome. Therefore it would be better to conduct two successful campaigns—let Burgoyne capture the lakes and the Hudson while Howe captured Philadelphia.

Having made this decision, General Howe seems to have become completely engrossed in his own campaign which involved the British victory at the Battle of the Brandywine on September 11, resulting in the capture of Philadelphia and the repulse of the strong American counterattack at Germantown on October 4. He forgot that as commander in chief of all the British armies in the colonies he was still responsible for Burgoyne's success or failure. He treated the operations as two entirely separate campaigns unrelated to each other. He did leave a force of about 7,000 men under the command of Lieutenant General Sir Henry Clinton in and around New York City to move northward if necessary, but then paid little attention to it for months.

It was not until after the capture of Philadelphia that Sir Henry Clinton moved to create a diversion to assist

Burgoyne. In 1777 the largest American strong points on the Hudson were Forts Clinton and Montgomery seven miles below West Point, which had not then been developed and fortified as the major stronghold of the Continental Army that it later became. Both of these forts were on the west bank of the river. The first was named for Brigadier General George Clinton, the American governor of New York who was at that time in command of the defense of both forts. (It is situated just south of the west end of the Bear Mountain Bridge in what is now a small state park; parts of the fort have been preserved or restored.) The second fort, named for General Richard Montgomery, killed in the assault on Quebec, was located a few hundred yards to the north across a deep ravine. Its commander was the governor's brother Brigadier General James Clinton. In addition to these forts a log boom and an iron chain stretched across the river to the eastern shore.

There were comparatively few soldiers available to defend either fort and both were taken on October 6, 1777, after brief but spirited engagements while the fleet passed over the chain and boom with little difficulty. The British then advanced as far north as Esopus (now called Kingston) which they burned on October 16. On the next day Burgoyne, far removed from his base and short of supplies, defeated at the Battles of Bennington and Saratoga and now surrounded by overwhelming numbers, surrendered. Sir Henry Clinton returned to New York, abandoning both Forts Clinton and Montgomery.

While these campaigns were in progress General Washington's actions presented an enlightening contrast to those of his adversary. In spite of the fact that he was completely involved in the campaign against General Howe, he never failed to keep the defense of northern New York in mind. Although outnumbered by the enemy in Pennsylvania, General Washington did not hesitate to send some of his best troops northward including Colonel Daniel Morgan's regiment of riflemen which played an outstanding part in the defeat of Burgoyne.

XI

The Saratoga Campaign

DURING the winter of 1776–1777 Major General John Burgoyne, who had been General Carleton's second in command in Canada, returned to England. His purpose was to gain the King's favor so that in the forthcoming campaign in America he would have a more important position than that of second in command. Upon arrival Burgoyne soon learned that both King George III and Lord George Germain were irritated at General Carleton for having retreated to Canada after the Battle of Valcour Island in October, 1776. He also discovered that Germain personally disliked Carleton and would be pleased to have someone else in command of the troops.

Burgoyne therefore found it quite simple to proceed; he did not even have to intrigue against Carleton. He submitted a paper to the King entitled "Thoughts for Conducting the War from the Side of Canada," then waited, feeling sure that his proposals would be adopted, not only because he felt they were militarily sound but also because of his skill as a writer. He had been a member of Parliament, had devoted much attention to art and drama, was a successful playwright, and believed himself to be a man of letters in addition to being a soldier. This idea would do him more harm than good in his dealings with the colonists, who did not appreciate and even laughed at his flamboyant style of writing.

Burgoyne's plan was to have three separate offensives converging on Albany. The main army under General Howe was to proceed north from New York City. Another large army, whose commander was purposely not named in the plan, was to move southward from Canada up Lake Champlain then cross to the Hudson River, while a third force was to move to Albany by way of Lake Ontario and the Mohawk Valley.

The King approved the plan and graciously indicated that Burgoyne should command the army moving from Canada via Lake Champlain. Lieutenant Colonel Barry St. Leger was eventually designated as commander of the third force with the temporary rank of brigadier general. General Carleton was to remain in Canada, charged with the defense of that province and with logistic support of the two columns advancing southward.

General Burgoyne returned to Quebec early in May, 1777. By mid-June an army of 7,850 men was concentrated near the northern end of Lake Champlain. Of these over 4,100 were British, nearly 3,100 were German; there were 250 Canadians and Tories plus about 400 Indians. At this time Burgoyne, using his new title of lieutenant general, issued a proclamation calling on the Loyalists to flock to the colors, offering protection to those who sided with the King, and threatening to turn his Indians loose on those who persisted in open rebellion. A few days later he made a speech to his Indian allies telling them that they must make war in a civilized manner; wounded and prisoners were not to be scalped or tortured; aged men, women and children must not be touched. All of this was announced in bombastic language which in the end caused laughter and ridicule not only in the colonies but also in the House of Commons in London.

Burgoyne would have been well advised to have forsaken the pen in favor of the sword. As a general he was ahead of his time in many respects. He believed in educating officers more thoroughly in their profession than was normal in the British army of the eighteenth century. He opposed cruel and unusual punishment, looked out for the health and spirit of his soldiers, and was popular with them. His nickname of "Gentleman Johnny" became a joke among the Americans but it meant quite the opposite to the British soldiers.

On June 18 the invading army and fleet sailed from near Plattsburgh, New York, up Lake Champlain and landed on July 1 north of Fort Ticonderoga on both sides of the lake; the Germans on the east, the British on the west. Major General Arthur St. Clair commanded the American garrison which consisted of a force numbering about 3,000 men. He had occupied and was defending the fort itself, Mount Independence across the lake, and another mountain called Mount Hope two miles to the northwest of the fort. He had failed to occupy Sugar Loaf (Mount Defiance), a mile to the southwest, which was by far the highest point in the area and dominated the fort and Mount Independence. It was considered to be inaccessible but Burgoyne was not so sure. On July 4 the British engineers and artillery started to work under the direction of Major General William Phillips, Burgoyne's second in command and a fine artilleryman. To encourage his men he announced that "where a goat can go, a man can go, and where a man can go he can drag a gun," then proceeded to prove it.

St. Clair immediately recognized his danger and on the night of July 5–6 evacuated Ticonderoga. The main body crossed to the east side of Lake Champlain, then headed south while the sick and wounded as well as some artillery and supplies were sent up the lake by boat to Skenesboro (now Whitehall), New York. A number of cannon and many valuable supplies were left behind to fall into the hands of the invaders.

Burgoyne sailed up Lake Champlain with the fleet and reached Skenesboro on the afternoon of July 6 in time to capture two ships; the remainder were burned as the Americans evacuated the post. Meanwhile Brigadier General Simon Fraser, followed by Major General Baron von Riedesel who commanded the German division, had started in pursuit of the main body. On the next day they surprised, and after a severe struggle, defeated the rear guard near Hubbardton, Vermont. General St. Clair managed to escape with the rest of his men and rejoined the army at Fort Edward, New York.

The fall of Ticonderoga was a great shock to the Americans; many people had believed that it was somewhat equivalent to Gibraltar, which of course had never been true even if there had been sufficient men present to garrison the place properly. General St. Clair, blamed for the defeat, was brought before a court of inquiry but was vindicated. He had been in command of the post only about two weeks and it had been General Horatio Gates, his superior officer, who had originally made the decision not to fortify Mount Defiance.

The King hailed the capture of Fort Ticonderoga with delight; it seemed that at last progress was being made toward conquering the colonies and restoring them to the Crown. Then Burgoyne made a fatal mistake. There were two routes by which he could reach Fort Edward on the Hudson. One was to continue overland via Fort Ann, a distance of 23 miles through a veritable wilderness of tall trees and deep ravines where roads were practically nonexistent. The other route was by way of Fort Ticonderoga, up Lake George and across country to a point on the Hudson above Fort Edward. This way presented difficulties also because falls and rapids in the waterway connecting the two lakes would require a portage of about 3 miles. However, there was a road of sorts between Lake

George and the Hudson and the distance was only 10 miles.

Apparently because he did not wish to appear to be retreating by returning to Ticonderoga to take the second and easier route, Burgoyne made the surprising decision to push his army straight ahead through the forest. Yet he sent his boats, his artillery and other heavy equipment over the portage into Lake George to rejoin him near Fort Edward.

Major General Philip Schuyler, the American commander in New York, promptly set his men to work felling trees and obstructing the road to Fort Edward in every possible way. The inhabitants were encouraged to drive off their horses and cattle and even burn their crops. It took Burgoyne's men three weeks to reach Fort Edward, an average rate of advance of a mile a day, yet under the circumstances this was quite an accomplishment in itself.

On August 3 Burgoyne received the shocking news that General Howe was not on his way to join forces at Albany but had started for Philadelphia. On that same day General Barry St. Leger, who had left Oswego on July 26, began the siege of Fort Stanwix (which is now within the city limits of Rome, New York). The army, if you can call it that, was a strange mixture. There were a few British regulars, some German troops, a number of Tories and a few Canadians, making a total of almost 900 white men. Their Indian allies added another 900 to the force. These were led by Chief Joseph Brant, the war leader of the Mohawks who were the most powerful tribe in the Iroquois League, or Six Nations, composed of the Mohawks, Onondagas, Cayugas, Senecas, Oneidas and Tuscaroras. Of these six the first four had now been persuaded to fight actively on the British side.

After a parade of his army in front of the fort to overawe the little garrison of only 750 men, St. Leger demanded a surrender. Colonel Peter Gansevoort and

J. Downey

CANADA
NEW YORK

St Lawrence

Plattsburgh

Valcour Island

BURGOYNE
7,850 Men

★ THE SARATOGA CAMPAIGN, 1777 ★

A Fort Ticonderoga, July 2-6
B Oriskany, Aug 6
C Bennington, Aug 16
D Freeman's Farm, Sept 19
   Bemis Heights, Oct 7

Lake Champlain

Fort
Ticonderoga
ST CLAIR
3,000 Men

Hubbardton

Whitehall
(Skenesboro)

Fort
Ann

Fort
Edward

Lake George

Hudson

VERMONT

ST LEGER
1,800 Men

Rome
(Fort Stanwix) 750 Men
Oriskany

HERKIMER
860 Men

Utica

Mohawk R

Schuylerville

Saratoga
Springs

ARNOLD
950 Men

Thruway
Schenectady

Bennington

Troy

Albany

VT

NEW YORK
MASS

Scale of Miles

0   10   20   30   40

Lieutenant Colonel Marinus Willett, who were in command, did not even deign to reply. They had no intention of letting that mob of savages loose in the Mohawk Valley by surrendering the main fort which guarded the entrance.

This is supposed to be the place where the Stars and Stripes first appeared in battle. There does not seem to be any doubt that it contained thirteen stripes, alternating red and white, but it is possible that instead of a circle of thirteen stars it contained the crosses of St. Andrew and St. George. The Stars and Stripes flag made by Betsy Ross was apparently intended originally for use on naval vessels rather than for the American army.

Three days later, August 6, 1777, Brigadier General Nicholas Herkimer, marching at the head of a column of 800 local militia and 60 friendly Oneida Indians to relieve Fort Stanwix, walked into an ambush near Oriskany, six miles from the fort. There ensued one of the most desperately fought battles ever recorded on the North American Continent. It was a bitter hand-to-hand struggle with tomahawks, clubbed muskets and knives, in which the number of killed far outnumbered the wounded. General Herkimer, wounded early in the battle, had himself carried into a small circle of fighting men and propped up against a tree to direct the battle. Finally the Indians decided it had lasted long enough and retreated; the Tories followed them back to the fort. The Americans also retreated; General Herkimer died a few days later.

The siege of Fort Stanwix continued. Lieutenant Colonel Willett and another man escaped from the fort to try to organize a second relieving force. They were met by the news that General Schuyler had already sent Benedict Arnold, now a major general, to save the garrison. Since he only had 950 men with him, Arnold first tried to frighten the Indians. He sent a half-witted German forward with an Indian companion to announce that Arnold was enroute with thousands of men. The Indians listened to him with the usual respect and awe they accorded to the insane, became alarmed, and fled. St. Leger perforce retreated to Oswego. This finished the third part of the British plan. With Howe gone to Philadelphia, Burgoyne was strictly on his own.

General St. Leger had begun his retreat to Oswego on August 22, but in the meantime other disasters had occurred to perplex Burgoyne. The first of these was a tragedy that happened on July 27, two days before his army reached Fort Edward. A party of marauding Indians had entered a cabin near the fort and taken two women prisoners. One was Mrs. McNeil, a cousin of the British General Simon Fraser. The other was Miss Jane McCrea, a young lady who was engaged to marry an officer in Burgoyne's army. On their return trip one of the Indians shot and scalped her. It is said that upon their arrival in the British camp at Fort Ann her fiance recognized the scalp. This immediately created an awful uproar throughout New York and New England. If a woman under the protection of the British Crown was not safe from the murderous savages, who could be safe? If there was one type of warfare in which the patriots excelled it was propaganda warfare. They made the most of it. Volunteers came flocking into the American camps.

Word also spread that General Gates had been chosen by Congress to supersede Schuyler in command of the army. This was good news to the people of New England, who blamed Schuyler for the loss of Ticonderoga and the subsequent retreat through the forest. Furthermore Schuyler was a wealthy landowner and thus represented the aristocracy of New York which was naturally suspect in New England. They trusted General Gates because as a former British officer he was supposed to know how to fight. Also they were well acquainted with his two principal subordinates, Major Generals Benedict Arnold of Connecticut and Benjamin Lincoln of Massachusetts.

The second and most serious disaster that fell to Burgoyne's lot also occurred before General Gates arrived to take command. Upon reaching Fort Edward the British had moved downstream a short distance and were then forced to halt to await supplies. Too much time had been consumed by hacking their way through the forest, and very little food and forage had been found enroute due to Schuyler's scorched-earth policy. It was decided to send a large force on a raid into the country to obtain horses and supplies.

XII

The Battle of Bennington

THE loss of Fort Ticonderoga and the British advance southward toward the Hudson alarmed the people in New England. They saw that they were in danger of being cut off from the other colonies and that their western frontier was being uncovered. It was now open to attack by Burgoyne, his Tories and his Indian allies.

The patriots living in the territory between New Hampshire and New York were particularly disturbed because they were nearest the enemy. Their land (now the State of Vermont) was then commonly known as the New Hampshire Grants because most of it had been settled by people from New England under grants of land made by the governor of New Hampshire. They had defied New York's claims to their territory for many years and now automatically looked to their own Green Mountain Boys to defend the land, and to New Hampshire for help.

In this emergency the choice of a leader was a foregone conclusion. John Stark, who had served in the French and Indian War in Rogers' Rangers, had made a name for himself defending the stone and rail fence at Bunker Hill, and had fought at Trenton and Princeton, was commissioned as a brigadier general of militia by New Hampshire. Stark accepted the appointment on the condition that he and his command would be independent of Congress and responsible only to the colony of New Hampshire. He was a brave, valiant soldier, a natural leader, but quick to resent an insult. When Congress passed several junior colonels over him and failed to appoint him as a general his pride had asserted itself and he had resigned. Now at the call of his colony he promptly began assembling the militia who responded eagerly when they heard that Stark would be their commander. By the first week of August, General Stark had organized and equipped a brigade of 1,500 men which he marched to Bennington, Vermont. Colonel Seth Warner, with 330 men, was left to guard Manchester, twenty-five miles to the north.

On August 11 the detachment whose mission was to obtain supplies, food, forage and horses for Burgoyne's army began its march. The force numbered 650 men and was composed of dismounted German dragoons, German grenadiers and light infantry, and a large percentage of Tories, Canadians and Indians plus a few British soldiers. The commanding officer was Lieutenant Colonel Friedrich Baum who could not speak a word of English. Since he was also supposed to meet a number of Loyalists sympathetic to the crown who would take up arms and fight for Great Britain, the choice of Colonel Baum and German mercenaries for such an expedition was certainly strange.

Their original destination was to be Manchester but at the last moment Burgoyne changed it to Bennington where large supplies were supposed to be stored and guarded by only a few militia. Equipped with this misinformation, Baum began a leisurely march to the southeast. His Indians caused trouble from the very beginning. Instead of rounding up cattle for food for the army, they slaughtered the animals just to keep the cowbells. The

news soon spread that the Indians were on the warpath,
so the horses and cattle were driven away, making Colonel Baum's task more difficult.

General Stark, discovering that there was a large force
following behind the Indians, sent word to Colonel Warner
at Manchester to join him, then marched to meet the
enemy. Colonel Baum also moved forward and at the
same time sent a messenger to Burgoyne asking for additional troops. On August 14 the two forces met but did
not become engaged. The 15th was rainy; again neither
side offered battle although each received some reinforcements. The Americans were increased to a strength of
2,000 militia including a few Indians, while Baum's detachment now numbered 800 men. General Burgoyne
had dispatched another force of 650 men under Lieutenant Colonel Heinrich von Breymann to support Baum,
but they did not arrive that day. Neither did Colonel
Warner's regiment from Manchester, but in spite of that
fact General Stark resolved to attack on the following day.

On August 16, the sun came out, the clouds broke
away, and both sides prepared for battle. By this time
the Americans knew precisely the strength and dispositions
of the enemy. Several men posing as friendly natives had
been scouting the enemy force. General Stark and Colonel
Warner—who had arrived in advance of his regiment to
learn the situation—prepared a rather complicated plan.
A column of 200 men under Colonel Nichols was to make
a long, flanking movement around to the north while
another of 300 men commanded by Colonel Herrick
made a similar march around to the south. An additional
300 men led by Colonels Hobart and Stickney were to
attack the nearest position east of the Walloomsac River.
When the flanking columns began their attack General
Stark was to launch the main assault with 1,200 men directly across the river toward the center of the enemy's
position.

The plan worked even better than could have been

expected. Colonel Baum was operating at a tremendous disadvantage. He had been informed that most of the natives in the area were Tories. When the flanking columns in the guise of small groups of farmers appeared about three o'clock in the afternoon he assumed they were coming to help him, until they opened fire at close range. Thereupon Colonels Hobart and Stickney advanced. The Canadians and Indians fled; the Tories ran after delivering one volley, leaving Colonel Baum at the main position on the high ground north of the river with only his German and British troops and a few other brave souls.

Stark gave the order to attack, shouting, "There they are! We'll beat them before the night, or Molly Stark will be a widow." The river was easily fordable and presented no obstacle, but the German dragoons on the hill resisted stoutly for two hours until their ammunition ran low and Colonel Baum fell mortally wounded. The first phase of the battle was over; the militia, disorganized by their victory, were scattered everywhere throughout the captured enemy camp. Then Colonel Breymann appeared on the scene leading the German reinforcements sent by Burgoyne.

Now it was General Stark's turn to worry. He hastily gathered a few men together and attempted to make a stand across the main road to the southwest but was soon forced backward. Here he was fortunately joined by Colonel Warner's regiment which had finally arrived on their march from Manchester. As other men appeared from the scene of the first battlefield Stark and Warner gathered enough strength to repulse the German attacks, then assault their enemy on both flanks. About sunset Colonel Breymann, wounded, with his coat shot full of bullet holes, and with his men's ammunition almost gone, ordered a retreat. The Americans undertook an immediate pursuit and pressed vigorously forward, and the retreat became a rout. The German drums beat the signal for a surrender conference but this noise meant nothing to the Americans who kept on firing until darkness put an end to the fighting.

The Americans lost about 30 killed and 40 wounded, while the German-British casualties were over 900 men killed, wounded and captured. (Although the battle was actually fought in New York, a majestic battle monument, 302 feet high, was erected to commemorate the victory in the town of Bennington, from which the battle derives its name, in the State of Vermont which furnished so many of the participants.)

It would be difficult to overestimate the effect of this battle upon Burgoyne's hopes and plans. Not only did he lose a large percentage of the troops under his command, but most of his Indians became disheartened and left. He did not dare send another detachment into the country to obtain supplies for fear it would meet a similar fate. Everything he needed must now come from Canada which meant a month's delay while he accumulated sufficient transport, equipment and supplies to proceed southward. Every day that Burgoyne was forced to wait in position the opposing American forces grew stronger as increasing numbers of patriots encouraged by the victory at Bennington joined the army.

XIII

The Battle of the Brandywine

NINE days after the Battle of Bennington, General Howe began landing his British and Hessian troops near the head of Chesapeake Bay, fifty miles from Philadelphia. By September 10 his army had marched as far as Kennett Square (on the present U. S. Highway No. 1), about halfway to its destination.

General Howe's advance had been terribly slow but there was nothing to guarantee that this would continue. He was now within easy striking distance of the capital; it was time to make a stand in its defense. Washington selected a position along Brandywine Creek directly across the line of advance toward Chester and Philadelphia. His force was outnumbered about 15,000 to 11,000, but he had found an excellent location. The Brandywine itself is not a formidable obstacle. There are numerous shallow fords throughout its length which could then (and still can) be easily recognized by the farm roads which lead to them. However, the valley is generally narrow and the crossing sites are dominated on each side by steep, wooded hills. Infantry posted on these hills would be difficult to assault and artillery could easily cover the fords with gunfire.

For the coming battle Washington organized his army into two wings. General Sullivan was placed in general command of the right wing, Greene in command of the left. Sullivan's force, the larger of the two, consisted of his own division and those of Stephen and Stirling. This wing was to cover the creek from Brinton's Ford northward (to where Street Road now crosses). Sullivan also sent small detachments farther upstream to guard against other possible crossings on the right flank.

The left wing stood astride the main route of advance at Chadd's Ford (on what is now U.S. No. 1) with General Anthony Wayne's Pennsylvania Continentals on the high ground just north of the ford, Greene's Virginians in the center, and about 1,000 Pennsylvania militia on the left at another ford about a mile and a half downstream. Washington stayed with the left wing and established his·headquarters in a house about a mile to the rear on the north side of the road. Lafayette, then a member of Washington's staff, occupied another house about a half mile farther to the rear beyond the Brandywine Church. (Both of these houses have now been carefully restored and furnished appropriately to the era as landmarks of the battlefield.)

In addition to the main army drawn up in line of battle along the creek Washington sent a small force of cavalry across to the west side along Street Road, and a selected force of about 700 light infantry under Brigadier General William Maxwell westward along U.S. No. 1 toward Kennett Square to gain contact with the enemy and delay his advance.

General Howe's army was also divided into two wings, one under General von Knyphausen, of about 5,000 men, the other of about 10,000 commanded by Cornwallis. About 4 o'clock in the morning of September 11, Cornwallis started marching from Kennett Square. After covering a little more than two miles the column turned left (4½ miles west of Chadd's Ford) and disappeared northward. Howe went with this, the larger of his two forces. So, entirely by accident, the larger wing of the British army which was on its left flank would eventually be opposed by the larger wing of the American army under Sullivan on the American right flank while the smaller wings would meet each other near Chadd's Ford.

Von Knyphausen's column kept straight ahead down the main road until it ran into Maxwell's light infantry about nine o'clock. The Americans delayed the advance for over an hour, forcing the head of the column to deploy, then falling back in successive delaying positions until forced across the Brandywine. Knyphausen then occupied the hills west of Chadd's Ford and made no further effort to advance but kept up an intermittent cannonade of the American lines.

This action by Knyphausen apparently accomplished exactly what it was supposed to do. It occupied Washington's attention but did not seem to arouse any suspicions as to what might be happening elsewhere. However, reports of other activities soon came from the right wing, forwarded by Sullivan, of enemy movements to his front northward toward the upper fords. At first Washington refused to believe that these were true, then becoming convinced, he concluded that Howe had made the mistake of dividing his army and decided to attack him. Washington actually issued orders for Sullivan to advance with the entire right wing, while Greene was to cross Chadd's Ford, when an entirely conflicting report was received that there was no enemy force threatening the right flank.

Although this latest report flatly contradicted the others and the weight of evidence was all in favor of the former, Washington guessed and guessed wrong that there was no enemy marching northward. He countermanded the orders for attack although some few of Greene's men were actually across the creek. The Americans then waited in their defensive positions.

It is difficult today to understand how Washington and

his advisers came to such a false conclusion and did not at least take some steps to determine more of what was happening to the north. Yet it is more difficult to visualize what might have happened if the army had attacked across the creek. The chances of success seem exceedingly slim, while if the attack had failed the result would have been a disaster far worse than the results of the actual battle.

In any event nothing happened until about two o'clock in the afternoon when an excited farmer named Thomas Cheyney rode furiously into Sullivan's camp to announce that the British were across the creek. Taken to Washington, he repeated his story again and again, but no matter how exasperated he became no one believed him. Then in dashed a courier from the cavalry, confirming the bad news. Hastily Sullivan was ordered to move the entire right wing back and face northward. Greene was to hold his division in readiness to move also if necessary; Wayne and Maxwell were to prepare to hold Chadd's Ford by themselves if Greene's troops were taken away.

At this particular moment the Americans were favored with a small amount of good fortune. It would take time to select a new position, move the troops to occupy it, and realign them to fight in an entirely different direction. By pure luck Cornwallis had chosen this hour to halt his troops. It was now 2:30 P.M. The British had been marching for over ten hours. The day had been exceedingly hot and the troops needed some rest and food before they advanced to battle.

By 3:30 Cornwallis was again ready to advance. His troops were now formed in three divisions on Osborne Hill. Facing them across a gently sloping valley about a mile and a half away on the next hill to the southeast, the Americans were hastily coming into position. One of the brigades from Sullivan's division was on the right flank, next was Stephen's division, then Stirling's, but Sullivan's second brigade was not yet in position. About four o'clock the British advanced straight across the valley and up the hill. At the very last moment Sullivan's second brigade arrived. In fact it was only beginning to form line on the left flank when it was struck by the British Guards and gave way in confusion. The brigade on the American right flank had also retreated hastily from the field. Thus Sullivan had only Stephen's and Stirling's division left to fight.

Washington, near Chadd's Ford, was now faced with a difficult decision. He could distinctly hear the sounds of battle to the north; Knyphausen to his front had made no move to attack. Should Greene's division stay where it was or move to Sullivan's aid? After some delay he decided that Greene must move and that he himself should hasten to the scene of battle. This was undoubtedly the correct decision. Wayne and Greene together could probably hold the ford against Knyphausen if he attacked, but if Sullivan and the right flank were driven back the battle was lost anyway. Washington set off across country with Greene and his division behind him. Lafayette, eager for battle, galloped ahead.

Knyphausen also heard the sound of the guns and knew that it was now time for him to play his part in General Howe's plan. As Greene's troops marched away from Chadd's Ford leaving only Wayne and Maxwell's light infantry, Knyphausen launched his assault. Thus assailed on two fronts, outnumbered on each, with Washington and Greene's division halfway between and able to render assistance to neither, the Americans fought grimly. The decision to move Greene had been correct but it had come too late.

Sullivan's men, five times driven from their position, counterattacked five times and regained their ground. They battled stubbornly, fighting with both flanks exposed and under attack, but inevitably were forced back in disorder. Cornwallis' center and left columns hastened to pursue, but his right column unaccountably kept

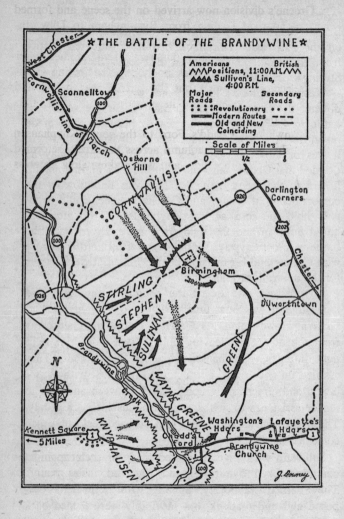

★ THE BATTLE OF THE BRANDYWINE ★

straight on toward the south; a move which soon proved fatal to Wayne's defense.

Greene's division now arrived on the scene and formed across the road leading from Birmingham to Dilworthtown, opening ranks to let the retreating soldiers through, then closing to face their pursuers. Here another bitter struggle ensued. There was no hope of defeating Cornwallis' victorious forces but the pursuit was halted and Greene was able to retire in good order at dusk, thus covering the retreat.

Meanwhile at Chadd's Ford to the south Knyphausen had pushed an assault column across the creek, reformed his lines on the other side, and was making slow progress against strong resistance. Wayne and his men were conducting a vigorous defense with some hope of success when suddenly they were struck in the right and rear by Cornwallis' wandering right column. This abruptly ended the defense of Chadd's Ford, but Wayne was able to disengage his force and retire slowly eastward, fighting delaying actions on successive hills until darkness covered his retreat.

The British casualties in killed, wounded, and missing in this battle were something less than 600 men. The Americans undoubtedly lost more; about 1,000 would seem to be a fair estimate. The Americans also lost eleven cannon which they could ill afford. Among the casualties was General Lafayette who was wounded in the leg but fortunately escaped capture.

That night the defeated Americans streamed along the road toward Chester with Wayne and Greene following to protect the rear. There Washington found the wounded Lafayette with a guard posted at a bridge, stopping the retreat. By the following day the army was ready to move and marched to protect Philadelphia. A fortnight of maneuvering followed. During this period General Wayne learned a few lessons about surprise attacks. On the night of September 20 Major General Charles

Grey led a British force in a bayonet charge with unloaded muskets into Wayne's camp near Paoli, Pennsylvania, twenty miles west of Philadelphia. In this engagement the Americans suffered about 300 casualties while the British had only 7 killed and wounded. It became known as the "Paoli Massacre" but there seems to be little factual evidence that it deserved to be called a massacre. General Wayne proved to be a very apt pupil, for just two years later he led a similar attack against the British at Stony Point, New York, with dramatic results.

On September 26 the British marched into Philadelphia; the loss of the Battle of the Brandywine had determined the fate of the city. At this time the capture of the colonial capital seemed a terrible blow to many patriots. It was the largest city in the colonies, with a population of 40,000. It ranked in size with the largest cities in England, next to London. Now both New York and Philadelphia were in British hands. General Howe believed that he had achieved an important objective, but neither Washington nor his army were discouraged. In fact they were already planning a counterstroke.

XIV

The Battle of Germantown

AFTER capturing Philadelphia, General Howe found himself faced with the problem of supplying his army. He had advanced overland to the city from near the head of Chesapeake Bay but this was far too long a route to maintain and guard against attack by marauding bands. In fact he had already been forced to detach 3,000 men for this purpose.

The obvious route for ships supplying Philadelphia was up the Delaware, but the Americans had obstructed its passage with obstacles in the water, guarded by various forts and redoubts. General Howe called on his brother the admiral to force a passage up the river, and sent troops to help. Cornwallis was left in command at Philadelphia. Howe established his camp six miles north of the city near the little village of Germantown. The strength of his army, reduced by these detachments, was about 9,000 men.

Washington determined to take advantage of this situation. He had received a few reinforcements after the Battle of the Brandywine and now outnumbered the British troops at Germantown. The American army was ready and eager to have another try at the enemy.

Germantown then consisted of little more than a double row of houses stretching for two miles on each side of the main road leading northwest from Philadelphia to Reading, fifty miles away. (The Germantown of today thickly populated and a part of the city of Philadelphia, bears no resemblance at all to that village of 1777. Fortunately for orientation purposes this road, then called the Skippack Road, coincides almost exactly with the present-day Germantown Avenue. Washington's army was encamped along this road sixteen miles from the village.)

The British were disposed on both sides of Germantown Avenue along a line facing northwest. Washington decided to make a surprise attack before daylight on this line of camps. The troops were to march sixteen miles in four separate columns, arriving at their assembly areas at 2:00 A.M., October 4, 1777. Precisely at 5:00 A.M. all four columns were to charge with bayonets fixed, without firing a shot. Each soldier was to have a piece of white paper pinned on his hat to identify him.

The two center columns were to deliver the main assaults while the two flanking columns were to simultaneously attack the rear of the British line on their north and south flanks. Even under the best of conditions with well-trained troops and modern communications, this would have been a difficult plan to execute. Separated by several miles of broken country, with no means of communication and with the flanking columns composed entirely of untrained militia, Washington's army would need a great deal of good luck on its side to carry out this elaborate plan successfully. As it turned out the attacking troops ran into one misfortune after another yet nearly won the battle because the British were not expecting an army so recently defeated at the Brandywine to return and attack so vigorously.

Of the two center columns, the first to arrive on the scene was that commanded by General Sullivan. It had

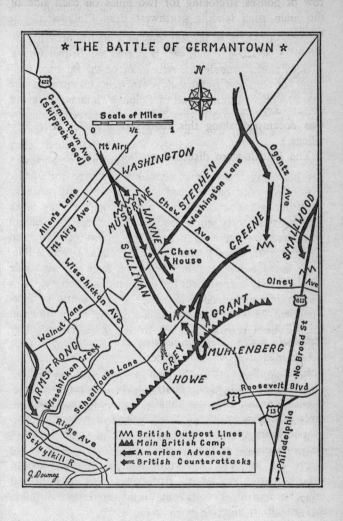

★ THE BATTLE OF GERMANTOWN ★

N

Scale of Miles
0   ½   1

Germantown Ave. (Skippack Road)

422

Mt Airy

WASHINGTON

Allen's Lane

Mt Airy Ave

Wissahickon Ave.

MUSGRAVE

WAYNE

STEPHEN

Chew

Washington Lane

Chew House

SULLIVAN

GREENE

SMALLWOOD

Ogontz Ave.

Olney   Ave.

611

GRANT

Walnut Lane

ARMSTRONG

Wissahickon Creek

Schoolhouse Lane

GREY

MUHLENBERG

HOWE

No Broad St.

Ridge Ave.

Roosevelt Blvd

Schuylkill R.

1

13

Philadelphia

J. Downey

British Outpost Lines
Main British Camp
American Advances
British Counterattacks

marched directly down the Skippack Road, and was followed by the reserve; Washington marched with this column. It struck a British picket near Mount Airy and quickly drove it back, but not in time to prevent the firing of two signal guns which alerted the British forces.

This alarm brought the remainder of the infantry regiment on outpost duty and some light infantry to the scene. Under the command of Colonel Thomas Musgrave they resisted so stoutly that Sullivan was forced to deploy his whole force, using his division on the west side of the road and Wayne's on the east side. Gradually they forced the British backward, but Musgrave was gaining for his army the time it needed to prepare for battle. The mist which had greeted the troops at sunrise thickened into a fog so dense that a man could not see more than thirty or forty yards. Under cover of this fog Colonel Musgrave was able to occupy the house of Benjamin Chew, former chief justice of Pennsylvania. It was a fine, large stone house standing well back from the east side of the road, surrounded by trees and shrubbery. It is the one remaining large landmark of the Battle of Germantown. This is quite appropriate, for its occupation and the stubborn resistance of its British defenders together with the prevailing fog proved to be the deciding factors in the battle.

Sullivan's and Wayne's men passed right on by the Chew House, leaving it to the attentions of the reserve. Instead of simply surrounding it and continuing forward, Washington decided—upon the advice of Brigadier General Henry Knox his chief of artillery—that the defenders must be forced to surrender before the reserve could safely proceed. The artillery opened fire, broke the front door, smashed the windows, destroyed the statuary and vases in the yard, but could not penetrate the thick, stone walls. Efforts to burn it failed.

General Greene's column, which contained more than half of the army, was now approaching from the north.

His men had marched four miles farther than Sullivan's, and in addition their guide had lost his way in the darkness, delaying the column for an hour. Greene marched onward, engaged the British outposts, drove them back and swept on toward the main line of resistance. But one of his divisions was missing. General Adam Stephen, hearing the cannonading at the Chew House, had turned aside without orders and marched toward that place. His artillery joined in the bombardment but the gallant defenders, completely surrounded, still hung on grimly to their stronghold.

General Wayne, hearing the increase in gunfire in his rear, thought that Sullivan was in trouble back there, wheeled about, and marched back to the Chew House. Upon his approach in the thick fog, Stephen's men mistook Wayne's soldiers for the enemy and started a battle between the two American divisions.

Sullivan and Greene were now left on their own, each operating independently of the other, but they pressed their attacks so vigorously that the British were actually contemplating withdrawal. At this juncture the British Generals Grant and Grey attacked Sullivan on both flanks, causing him to withdraw. They then turned on General Greene's division which was now in an unenviable position. One brigade commanded by Brigadier General John P. G. Muhlenberg, the gallant Lutheran pastor who said there is a time to preach and a time to fight, had penetrated the British line for more than a thousand yards and was now cut off. It turned about, and in a gallant charge reminiscent of Colonel Mawhood's breakout at Princeton, came back through the British line and joined Greene in his withdrawal.

This ended the main assaults of the two center columns. General William Smallwood, with the flanking force which was supposed to attack the British right rear from the northeast, had been given too long a distance to march over rough, broken country and did not arrive in time. When he reached the scene he wisely decided simply to turn around and rejoin the main army.

The other flanking column from the west, commanded by Brigadier General John Armstrong, had advanced along the Manatawny Road (or Ridge Avenue) to the junction of Wissahickon Creek and the Schuylkill River. From that point Armstrong opened fire on the British left, then decided to withdraw without committing his little force.

The troops engaged on each side numbered about 9,000 men. The British had over 500 killed and wounded, while the Americans lost over 1,000 killed, wounded and captured. By repulsing Washington's attack the British technically won the battle. The ultimate effect, although not fully appreciated by the colonists at the time, was quite the opposite. The leading statesmen and generals of Europe, particularly the French, were impressed by Washington's boldness and by the fighting ability of an army which could bounce back so rapidly from a defeat, take the offensive, and come so close to gaining a victory. When shortly thereafter the French government learned of the surrender of Burgoyne at Saratoga, the name Germantown helped influence its decision to form an alliance with the colonies.

XV

The Battles of Saratoga

WHEN Major General Horatio Gates arrived and assumed command of the northern American forces on August 19, 1777, he was greeted with enthusiasm by most of the officers and men of the army. He had acquired a well-deserved reputation as an able administrator, first as the adjutant general of the army, then in 1776 as the commander in upper New York who together with General Schuyler had helped provide Arnold with supplies and equipment to build the fleet which had fought at Valcour Island. Because Gates was from Virginia the soldiers from New England felt that they could trust him as they never had trusted General Schuyler. From the very beginning they had been prejudiced against Schuyler simply because he was from New York and represented the wealthy, aristocratic class in that colony. The soldiers from New York saw no reason to object to General Gates as a commander, because he had helped expel the enemy from their colony in the preceding year.

No one seemed to have stopped to consider the fact that Gates had never commanded a large force on a field of battle or the manner in which he had obtained his present appointment. This had been done by underhanded scheming in the halls of Congress at the expense of General Schuyler and with the assistance of various New England delegates.

General Gates could not possibly have selected a better time or place to assume command. Many of the problems which had faced General Schuyler were now solved. The Battle of Bennington, fought three days before, had immobilized General Burgoyne for an indefinite period until he could accumulate sufficient supplies to move southward. The American army was in a secure position just north of Albany where General Schuyler had brought it before turning over command. As a result of the murder of Jane McCrea by Indian allies of the British and the victory at Bennington, the colonial army was becoming stronger every day as volunteers came to join in ever increasing numbers. In the first week of September, General Benedict Arnold returned from his successful expedition against General Barry St. Leger, and Colonel Daniel Morgan arrived with his corps of riflemen from Washington's army. General Gates now felt strong enough to move northward toward his opponent. On September 12 (the day after the Battle of the Brandywine) the American army occupied a position on the west bank of the Hudson River at a place called Bemis Heights. On the following day General Burgoyne began crossing to the west bank of the Hudson at Saratoga (now Schuyler-ville) on his southward march toward Albany.

The position chosen by General Gates upon the advice of Benedict Arnold and the Polish engineer Thaddeus Kosciusko, who laid out the fortifications, was on a bluff rising steeply from near the water's edge to a height of over 100 feet. As the land stretched westward it rose even higher, reaching a height of 300 feet or more above the river. The main road running south to Albany passed through a narrow plain close to the water's edge and was completely dominated by the high ground above it.

The American defenses began at the riverbank and

followed the high ground of the bluff which overlooked the river to the east, a ravine to the north, and another smaller ravine to the west. The main fortifications therefore presented a three-sided appearance, each side over a half mile in length with the rear left open. At the northwest angle stood a house and a barn owned by John Neilson. The barn was strengthened and fortified as a key point in the American line and became known as Fort Neilson. (The Neilson House is today the only contemporary building still standing near the battlefield.)

General Gates apparently intended to fight the coming battle from these fortifications, relying upon their strength and the ability of his men to repulse a direct assault. As the battle developed however there were two other terrain factors which were far more important to the outcome. The first of these was some higher ground farther to the west which was not occupied by the Americans. If the British could seize this ground and emplace their artillery on it they could dominate the American position. In fact this high ground was the ultimate objective of the British in both of the Battles of Saratoga.

The other feature was the character of the terrain stretching northward from the American position. It presented quite a different appearance than it does today; there were at that time only a few small clearings surrounded by tall trees and thick woods. The roads were mere wagon tracks or trails cut through the forest. This ground was particularly well suited to the American frontier style of fighting. The British and Germans would not be able to make much use of their preferred methods of advancing in close ranks, firing by volleys, and direct mass attacks with the bayonet.

The Battle of Freeman's Farm: About ten o'clock in the morning of September 19, 1777, General Burgoyne advanced toward the American position. His army now numbered only 6,000 men of which he planned to use 4,200 in the attack, keeping 1,800 to guard his boats and supplies and act as a reserve. The 4,200 men were to move forward in three columns. The strongest column was to be on the right, or the west end of the line. It was commanded by Brigadier General Simon Fraser and contained some 2,000 men; its objective was the unfortified high ground overlooking the American defenses from the west. The center column of 1,100 men was commanded by Brigadier General James Hamilton. The left column near the river was led by Major General von Riedesel and also numbered about 1,100 men. Burgoyne marched with the center column while General William Phillips, his second in command, went with the left column.

Since General Fraser's troops had to march a considerable distance before they could get into position, the other two columns were halted in place until about 1:00 P.M. when three guns were fired as a signal for the army to advance.

So for three hours, from ten in the morning until one in the afternoon, the American scouts kept reporting to General Gates the movements of the enemy which they could see plainly through the trees. During all this time Gates did nothing until finally, yielding to Arnold's pleas, he sent Morgan and the riflemen to oppose the flanking movement which threatened the position from the west. From the very beginning General Arnold saw clearly the advantage of fighting the British in the woods before they reached the main position.

In a ravine south of Freeman's Farm, Morgan's men drove back a group of the enemy, advanced forward, then were driven back themselves. Morgan rallied his men who responded to the turkey call which he sounded to assemble them. With the aid of two other regiments of Continentals he formed a line along the south edge of Freeman's Farm, a clearing covering about fifteen acres.

At this point General Arnold assumed command of the American troops on the left and brought more men into line. He soon noticed that there was an interval between

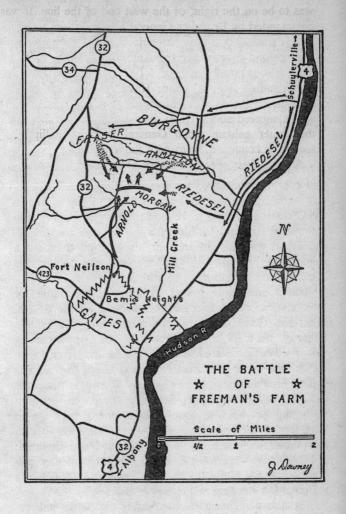

THE BATTLE
OF
FREEMAN'S FARM

Scale of Miles

J. Downey

the British right, or west column, and the British center column. Leading his men in an impetuous rush, he strove to smash into the gap. The British lines on both sides bent inward but the Americans could not break through. Then back and forth across the clearing the lines surged in some of the hardest fighting of the war. Arnold felt certain that with reinforcements he could break the line, but Gates refused to send any until late in the afternoon when he sent one brigade which instead of helping Arnold made an ineffective attack upon the enemy right flank.

While the battle was raging General Phillips rode over from the left column, advancing near the river, to lend a hand. But it was General von Riedesel, commanding that column, who saved the day for Burgoyne. Throughout the campaign this stalwart soldier who had served in the German armies for more than twenty years had proved a tower of strength. In this crisis, on his own responsibility, he stopped the advance of his column, detached a reinforced regiment, and led it personally against the American right, causing it to withdraw.

Arnold and Morgan had nearly won the battle for the Americans. Von Riedesel had saved it for the British. What had Gates done? He could have won the fight in either of two ways; by reinforcing Arnold or by attacking von Riedesel's isolated column beside the river. With 4,000 men under his direct command Gates had sat idle behind his fortifications, leaving Arnold to fight the battle with 3,000 men of whom only a portion were continuously engaged because Gates held so many back for so long. The Americans lost over 300 casualties. The British had about twice as many killed, wounded and captured; most of them were from General Hamilton's center column which had borne the brunt of the battle. One British regiment lost over three-quarters of its men.

The Battle of Bemis Heights: After the Battle of Freeman's Farm, General Burgoyne planned to resume the attack but changed his mind when he received word from

General Sir Henry Clinton that he was planning a move northward from New York City. The decision to wait for Clinton proved fatal, as the diversion provided came too late and was ineffective.

While waiting Burgoyne strengthened his position by erecting redoubts, digging trenches, and chopping down trees to provide a field of fire in front of his position. The two most important redoubts were near the west end of the British line. The one near Freeman's Farm where the line curved to the north is known as the Balcarres Redoubt, named for the Earl of Balcarres, a major whose British light infantry were posted there. The other, farther to the north, was held by Lieutenant Colonel Heinrich von Breymann and his German troops. (This redoubt now bears his name.) Both of these forts became well known as a result of the second battle fought here, which is usually referred to as the Battle of Bemis Heights but is also called the Second Battle of Freeman's Farm or the Battle of Stillwater.

While the British were strengthening their line the Americans made haste to correct the error in their defenses by occupying and fortifying the higher ground to the west which had been Burgoyne's objective on September 19. With both sides at work on their fortifications it might seem that a stalemate had been reached, but this was not at all the case. The American forces were still increasing in strength daily. Major General Benjamin Lincoln, who had been operating on the east side of the Hudson, brought his men across. By early October the Americans could count as many as 11,000 men. On the other hand, Burgoyne's supplies were not reaching him, the men's rations were reduced, horses died of starvation; his effective strength could not have been much more than about 5,000 men.

Burgoyne decided to make one last effort to get around the American army. On October 7 he sent out a reconnaissance in force of some 1,600 men, hoping to find a

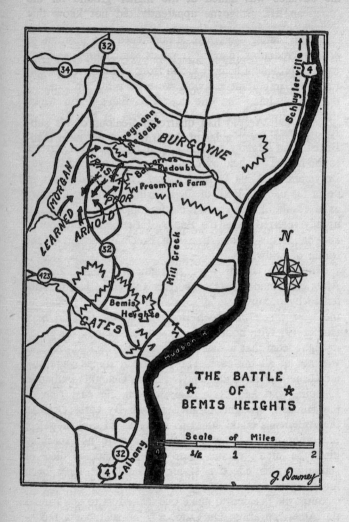

THE BATTLE
OF
BEMIS HEIGHTS

Scale of Miles

J. Downey

weak point in his opponent's line. As in the first battle, the advance was aimed at the higher ground on the American left. Burgoyne apparently did not know this position had now been fortified. The venture proved to be a very unsound move, since the force was large enough to invite a concentrated attack but too small to defend itself properly against such an assault. There was only one circumstance that favored it, but this was none of Burgoyne's doing.

Gates and Arnold had quarreled. Jealous of his subordinate, the commander of the army had not even mentioned Arnold in his report to Congress of the previous battle. This had led to a bitter exchange, and as a result Arnold had been deprived of his command and was sulking in his tent. Fortunately for the American cause he did not leave the area but remained in case there was another battle in which he might take part.

Burgoyne's reconnaissance in force was soon discovered. After advancing a short distance and finding nothing, it halted in a wheatfield with its flanks resting against thick woods. Gates sent Morgan forward to break out from the woods on the west and Brigadier General Enoch Poor to attack from the east. Having the shorter distance to go, Poor launched his assault first; Morgan then assailed the west flank. At this juncture in defiance of his orders, Arnold rode into the conflict leading three regiments of General Ebenezer Learned's brigade in an advance on the center of the British force.

With their flanks recoiling and their center about to give way, the British fought valiantly, inspired by the example of their leader, General Simon Fraser, who rode back and forth on his horse encouraging the men. Recognizing the importance of this officer who was sustaining the British in their defense, Arnold directed Morgan to have his rifle marksmen shoot him. Whereupon Morgan selected Tim Murphy to fulfill the assignment; at the third shot Fraser fell mortally wounded. The reconnaissance in force collapsed as the men retreated to their prepared fortifications.

The average general would probably have been willing to call it a day. The enemy had been thrown back into his entrenchments but the team of Arnold and Morgan was not finished. While Colonel Morgan marched his riflemen on a wide circuit around the British right Arnold led an attack against the Balcarres Redoubt. But in spite of all he could do, leading the men and exposing himself time and again with the utmost bravery, the defense proved too strong.

Whereupon seeing General Learned's brigade approaching on his left, Arnold galloped madly toward them between the lines of the two opposing armies firing at each other. Miraculously he survived this gauntlet of fire, took charge of the brigade, and swept forward between the Balcarres and Breymann Redoubts. Then turning to the north, he took command of all the troops in the area and stormed the Breymann Redoubt while Morgan's men came in from the other side. As Arnold victoriously led the way, sword in hand, he was shot in the left leg, the bullet fracturing his thigh. It was the same leg that had been wounded at Quebec. (On the battlefield there is an unusual monument commemorating Arnold and his achievements. The United States could not erect a monument to the traitor Benedict Arnold, so simply honored the memory of his gallant leadership at Saratoga by a memorial to his wounded leg.)

After the capture of this redoubt and the loss of their leader Colonel Breymann, who fell mortally wounded in its defense, the Germans made an attempt to regain it but were repulsed. Darkness brought an end to the battle, and for all practical purposes to the campaign. With his position now open to attack from the right rear, Burgoyne had only one course of action open to him. He began his retreat that night. On this day of battle Burgoyne lost about 600 men killed, wounded and captured, while the American loss was only 150 men.

Ten days later on October 17, 1777, surrounded by an army which had now increased to a strength of 20,000 men, the British laid down their arms. A total of over 5,700 officers and enlisted men surrendered. This event marked the turning point of the Revolution. France, which had been surreptitiously aiding the colonists, now came out openly on their side. King Louis XVI promptly approved an alliance, and on February 6, 1778, a formal treaty was signed. Soon thereafter Great Britain and France were at war. Spain eventually followed France, and before long England was also at war with Holland.

XVI

From Saratoga to Monmouth

SHORTLY after Burgoyne's surrender at Saratoga some
of Washington's soldiers found themselves engaged in a
fierce struggle along the Delaware just south of Philadelphia. General Howe and his brother Admiral Howe
had already begun operations to force a passage up the
river so that it could be used as the main supply line to
the troops in the city. They had not yet reached the
principal American fortifications, which were Fort Mercer on the heights at Red Bank on the New Jersey shore,
and Fort Mifflin which was then on an island called Mud
Island in the river. Together the two forts defended the
ship channel and the obstacles placed in the water.

The first attack against the forts came on October 22,
1777, when Colonel Carl von Donop led 2,000 Hessians
against Fort Mercer. It was held by only 400 Rhode
Island Continentals commanded by Colonel Christopher
Greene. The attacking Hessians were repulsed with heavy
losses, among them Colonel von Donop who was mortally wounded. On the same day the Royal Navy attempted a bombardment of the forts and lost two
warships.

The British then began a siege of Fort Mifflin. First

they constructed batteries on adjacent islands, which required a major effort on their part. The islands were little better than mudbanks with a few scattered humps of dry land. November brought cold weather, strong winds and thick ice. The batteries were built so close to the fort that all work had to be done under cover of darkness.

The British next brought up a floating battery, and on November 10 opened fire. For six days they shelled the little fort continuously at a range of 600 yards or less. On November 15 the Royal Navy brought several ships to add their fire to the overwhelming weight of metal that poured upon the defenders who gave up the hopeless struggle that night. The survivors escaped across the river to New Jersey. Fort Mercer was also evacuated; it would have been hopeless to attempt to defend it.

The prolonged defense of these two forts deserves more than the passing mention usually accorded it in our history books. This is unfortunate because the determined defenders not only gave a good account of themselves, holding their positions far longer than could reasonably have been expected, but also prevented General Howe from undertaking active operations against Washington's army for a period of over a month. It was not until December that Howe ventured forth. The results were inconclusive. The British went into winter quarters in Philadelphia while Washington chose Valley Forge.

It was also unfortunate at this time that people who should have known better were beginning to compare Washington very unfavorably with Gates. The city of Philadelphia and the water approach to it had been lost; the battles of Saratoga had been won. Washington was a failure, Gates a success. The near miracles of Trenton and Princeton were conveniently forgotten by Washington's enemies, and he had of course made a few enemies over the years. In addition, the victor at Saratoga seemed to have convinced himself that he was a better general than his commander in chief, although Morgan's riflemen must have told quite a different story as soon as they returned to the army in Pennsylvania.

It would be unfair to blame General Gates for starting an intrigue against Washington, although when he sent the news of Burgoyne's surrender to Congress he did ignore the commander in chief, leaving Washington to find out about it later. For several months there had been a movement underway in Congress and within the army itself to discredit Washington and if possible cause him to resign.

This conspiracy had become known to history as the "Conway Cabal," named for Thomas Conway, its most active spirit, an Irish adventurer who had served in the French army and had obtained the rank of brigadier general in the colonial army. Several Congressmen were involved and a number of army officers; the most important of these in addition to Gates and Conway were Major General Thomas Mifflin and Lieutenant Colonel James Wilkinson, one of General Gates' staff officers.

Of course Washington knew of the existence of the conspirators. In fact it became difficult to ignore their overt actions and hostile speeches after a while. Insulting letters were brought to his attention, and in one such instance Washington sent an extract in a short note to General Conway which thoroughly frightened the latter. This should have been enough to have stopped the movement but the ringleaders were soon more vociferous than ever.

Meanwhile in spite of the threat to his future, Washington maintained his dignity and poise, refusing to allow himself to be drawn into any controversy, but continuing to do his best to fulfill his duties as commander in chief. So much has already been written about the suffering endured that winter that the very mention of Valley Forge should be enough of a description; the name itself has almost come to mean endurance against hunger, cold and misery. For the third year in a row Washington had

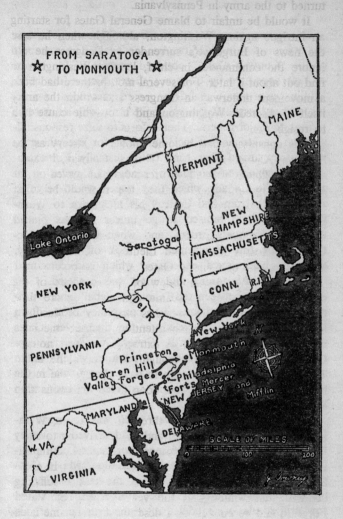

FROM SARATOGA
☆ TO MONMOUTH ☆

MAINE

VERMONT

NEW
HAMPSHIRE

Lake Ontario

Saratoga

MASSACHUSETTS

NEW YORK

CONN.

R.I.

Del. R.

New York

N

Princeton · Monmouth
Barren Hill ·
Valley Forge · · ·
Philadelphia
Forts Mercer
NEW JERSEY and
Mifflin

PENNSYLVANIA

MARYLAND

DELAWARE

SCALE OF MILES

0   100   200

W. VA.

VIRGINIA

to stand by and watch the army dissolve as death and desertion took their toll; then again build a new army to take the place of the former one.

During this winter of 1777–78 the conspiracy against the commander in chief reached its peak. The members of the "Conway Cabal" obtained control of the Board of War appointed by Congress. Gates became the head. Mifflin was a member and the Board succeeded in making Conway inspector general of the army with an increase in rank to major general. Their efforts to seize responsibility then proved to be their undoing, for everything to which they turned their hand failed dismally. For example, they conceived the idea of sending Lafayette on an expedition to Canada which they hoped would serve to separate him from and destroy his allegiance to Washington. Lafayette refused to go unless he was placed under Washington's orders, and when Congress reluctantly made this arrangement he took off for Albany. Here the harebrained expedition which had consumed two months of planning and effort was canceled.

The contrast between the "Conway Cabal" and Washington became too obvious. The conspiracy broke down while the members quarreled among themselves. Gates was finally sent back north. General Greene was appointed quartermaster general, a position which Mifflin had previously occupied; this was a change which the army soon appreciated. Conway tendered his resignation and it was promptly accepted.

In February a foreign officer who was to prove invaluable to the Continental cause had arrived at Valley Forge. Eventually appointed inspector general, the position made vacant by Conway's resignation, Major General Baron von Steuben undertook the task of drilling the army in the snows of Valley Forge. He formulated new drill regulations modeled after the Prussian methods of Frederick the Great, but greatly modified and adapted to the American temperament and conditions of warfare in the colonies. This would have been a terrific job for anyone, but von Steuben was more than handicapped by his lack of knowledge of English. Often at drill his command of the language failed and he would plead with others to swear at the troops for him. His idiosyncrasies delighted the soldiers, who then worked all the harder for him. His training methods particularly varied from those of the British Army by placing greater responsibility on the junior officers; a challenge they rose to meet. When Washington broke camp at Valley Forge his newly trained army was the best he had ever put in the field.

With the coming of spring the effect of the treaty of alliance signed with France in February, 1778, began to be felt, first on the sea, then on land. Ammunition, guns, supplies of all kinds no longer needed to be obtained secretly without the official knowledge of King Louis XVI. French seaports were now open to American ships of war and to privateers. Captain John Paul Jones, commanding the sloop *Ranger*—the first warship to fly the new Stars and Stripes adopted by Congress—had sailed for France in November, there to become the center of an international controversy. When France became an ally his ship was openly received, and in Quiberon Bay had the distinction of being the first armed vessel to receive a foreign salute to the new American flag. In April Captain Jones set sail to harry the coasts of England and Ireland, bringing the war closer home to the enemy, and in the process capturing the British sloop *Drake*.

In April also, Admiral Comte d'Estaing sailed from France for American waters with a large fleet. The British had been having trouble enough over the past two years contending against the increasing losses of merchant ships to American privateers. Now they would have to face the additional menace of large numbers of enemy warships. Their convoys would have to be more closely guarded, and they could no longer move their armies so easily back and forth along the coast without fear of meeting a hostile fleet. Sea power in the American Revolution was no longer a one-sided affair.

Early in May the Congress ratified the treaty with France, and Lieutenant General Sir Henry Clinton arrived in Philadelphia to relieve Howe as commander in chief of the British forces. However there was a delay in making the change, and Howe was given one last chance at a portion of the American army. General Lafayette had been put in command of about 2,200 men (almost a third of the strength of the army at that time) and been sent forward as a security guard to obtain intelligence of the enemy's movements.

Lafayette took an exposed position at Barren Hill, about halfway between Valley Forge and Philadelphia, which placed his forces in a dangerous position. General Howe set a trap for him, to be sprung early in the morning of May 20, 1778. But a gallant and intrepid American captain named Allen McLane who had led many of the scouting and foraging parties during the winter at Valley Forge, discovered the move in time. When the trap was sprung the quarry was gone. But it was a good test of the training of the new American army and one which they passed with flying colors. Shortly afterward Clinton superseded Howe.

The new commanding general had orders to evacuate Philadelphia and return to New York. It had finally been recognized by the British government that, although Philadelphia was the capital city, for the main army to remain where it was would in no way lead toward the destruction of Washington's army, the prime objective. In fact, now that Burgoyne's army had surrendered, the army in Philadelphia was actually nothing more than a large isolated garrison.

The orders to evacuate the capital were simple to give but not to execute. Now that France had entered the war communications by sea were very vulnerable;

the arrival of a large French fleet could destroy the army
en route. Furthermore the army was too large and had
accumulated too much baggage and there were not enough
transports to make the voyage by sea in one convoy. So
Clinton decided to march the larger part of the army overland, sending most of his impedimenta and the civilians
who wished to leave the city, by ship to New York.

XVII

The Battle of Monmouth

ON June 16, 1778, General Clinton began the evacuation of Philadelphia. Two days later Captain Allen McLane and his band entered the city and reported to Washington that the British were gone. It is possible that the Continental army missed a grand opportunity to destroy a large portion of the enemy while the force to go through New Jersey was crossing the Delaware. But at that time Washington had been calling councils of war to decide what to do, and General Charles Lee, the respected second in command who had recently been exchanged as a prisoner of war, was strongly opposing any attack, saying that Americans could not stand against British regulars.

It was however decided to harass Clinton on his march. To that end General Philemon Dickinson's New Jersey militia and General William Maxwell's New Jersey Continentals were asked to annoy the enemy by hanging on his flanks, obstructing roads, and cutting bridges. By June 23 Washington's army was across the river; it totaled some 13,500 including those harassing Clinton. Then more men were detached for this purpose including Morgan's riflemen and General Enoch Poor's New Hampshire brigade, all under the command of Brigadier General

146

Anthony Wayne. It was thereupon decided that a major general was needed to command the whole force. June 25, 1778, was a fateful day for the American army. When first offered that major general's command of the advancing forces, Lee had refused and Lafayette had delightedly accepted. Then later Lee, realizing how important an assignment it really was, demanded that it be given to him, and Washington agreed because of Lee's position in the army.

On the same day, June 25, General Clinton changed his line of march toward Monmouth Court House (now the town of Freehold, New Jersey). Fearful of attack on his long, plodding column of 15,000 men, he veered away to the northeast, farther away from Washington who was on his left, west flank. Although Clinton had a headstart, his progress had been incredibly slow. The weather was excessively hot and humid with frequent downpours. His men were burdened with eighty-pound packs, and their fancy uniforms were soggy and painful to wear. Furthermore he was hauling an immense baggage train of 1,500 wagons; the roads had been obstructed; bridges had to be constantly repaired; and the forces on his flanks had continually annoyed and delayed his progress. Also he knew that Washington's men had been traveling light and fast.

Two days later on June 27 Lee was given orders to attack the British rear guard, which lay near Monmouth Court House, on the following morning. The idea was that if this proved profitable the whole army would be employed. Lee gave no orders for the attack, claiming lack of information of the enemy, and went to bed for the night.

Clinton was much more active; he was in a hurry to get away. At four o'clock in the morning of June 28 he sent off Von Knyphausen's division followed by the baggage train; Cornwallis' rear division was to follow. The latter, a larger force holding the post of honor in this case, contained the very best in the army: three fine British brigades, the Guards, two battalions of British grenadiers and the Hessian grenadiers, two battalions of British light infantry, the 16th Dragoons and Colonel Simcoe's Tory Queen's Rangers.

Word of Von Knyphausen's movement was brought by General Philemon Dickinson and his militia to Lee and to Washington. The former did nothing, but Washington ordered him to attack. Here was the first grand opportunity to test the new American army in battle. The value of the long hours of drill under Von Steuben's watchful eye, all the work of the winter and spring would culminate here. The British and Hessian regulars would learn that an American army second to none had come into being.

But of all the people in the world, General Charles Lee, who did not believe that anything could stand against British bayonets, was the last one who should have been given the job. The American columns were in motion by seven o'clock in the morning. Three hours later, after a couple of skirmishes and much hesitation, about 6,000 troops had reached a general line north of the town of Freehold and south of that portion of McGellairds Brook known to history as the East Ravine. The fact that they had reached a position from which an attack could be launched upon the enemy was no credit to General Lee. He had issued orders, then followed them with contradictory orders, while some troops received none at all. Morgan's riflemen, for instance, three miles away, received nothing and missed the battle entirely. On the hills north of Freehold the proverbial "Order, Counterorder, Disorder" prevailed. Lee not only had no plan of attack but had lost control of the advance.

At this juncture General Clinton, fearful for the safety of his army and its long baggage train, turned to attack and drive the Americans away. Filled with dread of the British bayonets, or as some say filled with treachery, General Lee ordered a retreat. Sullenly the troops with-

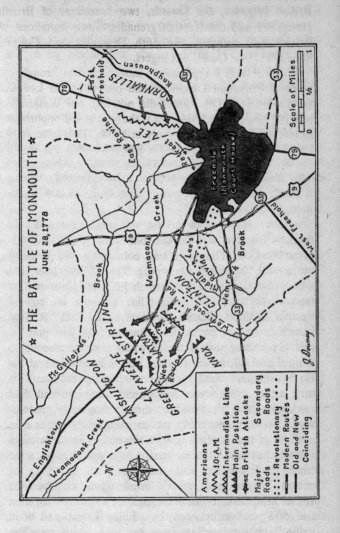

drew from a battle they had not even been permitted to try to fight, but thanks to the drill at Valley Forge there was no panic or rout. Slowly, resentfully, they marched back through dust and appalling heat; the thermometer now stood at 97° in the shade and would go higher before the day was over.

Washington, riding in advance of the main body, met the retreating troops somewhere on this road. At first he could not believe what they told him; one poor soldier was temporarily placed in arrest for spreading false rumors. Regimental and brigade commanders could tell him nothing; some had orders to retreat, others were simply following because it seemed to be expected of them. All were filled with anger rather than fear. At last Washington met Lee.

For the second time in the war the commander in chief lost his temper (the first had been at Kip's Bay). Accounts of what actually happened vary and most of them sound too stilted to be accurate. Many agree that as he ordered Lee to the rear they heard him mutter "damned poltroon." But the best account is that of Brigadier General Charles Scott who said that "on that memorable day he swore like an angel from Heaven!"

Hastily issuing orders to the main body to deploy to the right and left of the road and form a new line to the rear, Washington went forward to stop the retreat. This was a much more severe test of the discipline and drill of the new army than had even been originally contemplated. To turn retreating troops completely around in the midst of that confusion, with the enemy in some cases no more than two hundred yards away, would require the utmost in leadership and training. With the help of General Wayne and others Washington managed to form an intermediate line with some of the retreating men on a good position between the Middle Ravine and West Ravine. The intermediate line was to hold, if possible, long enough so that the new line could be organized.

Greene, back with a division, commanded on the right of the new line, Stirling on the left, with Lafayette in charge of the reserve.

Without hesitation the British charged forward into the hastily forming intermediate positions, and severe fighting ensued. On this extremely hot, oppressive day it is not hard to understand why the presence of Molly Pitcher carrying water to her husband's gun crew was so welcome. It was here that, when he fell mortally wounded, she grabbed the rammer and bravely served the gun in his place.

Slowly Wayne and his men were pressed back across the West Ravine where they clung to a position along a hedge by an orchard in front of the center of the new line. Clinton then attacked Stirling's division north of the road and was flung back after a fierce struggle. His next attempt was directed against the American left, south of the road, but here Greene had forestalled him by moving a body of troops and cannon around to a hill on the south flank. The combined frontal fire of Greene's division and the enfilading cannonfire directed by General Knox in person on Clinton's left flank stopped this attack.

A third attack against Wayne's troops in the center failed. Then a full hour passed while Clinton organized a final assault, again at the center. This was too large for Wayne to halt alone. His men fell back on the main position which by now was too strong for the British to hope to carry. About six o'clock in the evening Clinton withdrew his forces. Washington attempted to form a counterattack but darkness came before he could execute it. The next morning the British and Hessians were gone, on their way to New York.

Both sides claimed a victory at the Battle of Monmouth and with equal justice. Of 9,500 men engaged, the British and Hessians suffered a loss of about 350 killed, wounded and missing, including 59 dead from fatigue and heat prostration. The entire American army of 13,500 was engaged and lost about the same number, including 37 dead from sunstroke.

This battle has been classified as indecisive because both sides claimed to have won. This is true only in a limited sense. After the battle Clinton moved to New York, and Washington to the Hudson above that city. So after two years of battles, campaigns and privations, both armies were right back where they had started. But the differences in their situations, between 1776 and 1778 were striking. The British had failed in their effort to conquer the northern colonies. They abandoned hope of defeating the new, well-trained American army which had proved its worth at Monmouth, and thenceforth turned their major efforts toward conquering the south.

An important result of the battle was that it ended the career of the troublemaker General Charles Lee. He was tried by court-martial, found guilty, and suspended from command for twelve months. This sentence was approved by the Congress, whereupon some months later Lee wrote an insulting letter to the Congress which then expelled him from the army.

XVIII

From Monmouth to Camden

ADMIRAL d'Estaing and his fleet arrived just too late
to catch Clinton's convoy en route to New York. Then
the admiral discovered that the water was too shallow
for his ships to get at the British fleet in New York
Harbor. So the question arose as to what to do with the
French fleet and with the army of 4,000 soldiers which
d'Estaing had brought. All these allies could not be left
idle after coming all the way from France to help the
Americans in their revolution.

At this time the British had only two major seaports
under their control. New York was too heavily garrisoned to be attacked, but Newport, Rhode Island, was
a possibility. It had been in British possession since December, 1776, and was now occupied by only 3,000 men
commanded by General Sir Robert Pigot.

General John Sullivan, in command in Rhode Island,
had about 1,000 Continental soldiers. At his call about
6,000 militia arrived to help, and Washington sent him
3,000 more Continentals, making a total force of 10,000
troops. The initial landing efforts of both allies early
in August, 1778, were somewhat unco-ordinated, and the
American militia were late in arriving. Then Admiral

Howe arrived with a larger fleet. Fortunately for the French a great storm arose, dispersing both fleets; Howe returned to New York to refit.

Sullivan then attacked Pigot, but when d'Estaing returned with his fleet and his troops he refused to co-operate and sailed away to Boston to refit his ships. This caused the militia to desert in droves, leaving Sullivan in a precarious position. He managed to withdraw, late in the month of August; a movement in which a colored regiment from Rhode Island under Colonel Christopher Greene fought exceptionally well. The result of this first effort of the Americans and French to co-operate had therefore resulted in a fiasco which caused a great deal of ill feeling.

Admiral d'Estaing departed for the West Indies. General Clinton also sent a large force there, leaving the American scene to a comparative quiet for the winter as far as Washington's army was concerned, except for the territory near New York City where numerous small raids occurred, keeping the inhabitants in continual fear.

It is most difficult to present in chronological order, without confusion, the operations of Washington's troops, the fighting on the Indian frontiers, and the war in the South. We will therefore depart somewhat from the strict order of events to describe the story of George Rogers Clark and the Old Northwest.

Throughout the Revolution the settlers in what is now Kentucky, West Virginia and Western Pennsylvania were continually tormented by Indian raids. The British aided and abetted these from their main base at Detroit. The agent there was Lieutenant Colonel Henry Hamilton, known far and wide as "the Hair Buyer" because he paid the Indians for white scalps.

In 1777 Colonel George Rogers Clark, the elder brother of William Clark, later famous for his part in the Lewis and Clarke Expedition of 1804–06, conceived the idea of striking at the Indians in the Illinois territory.

From Patrick Henry, then governor of Virginia, he received some money and permission to raise troops for the purpose.

In May and June, 1778, Clark managed to gather together a few riflemen at the Falls of the Ohio (Louisville, Kentucky). Near the end of the month he set out with 175 men, and surprising the inhabitants, seized Kaskaskia without firing a shot. Cahokia also fell into his hands without resistance. Then Father Pierre Gibault of Kaskaskia persuaded the people of Vincennes to join the American cause. A detachment occupied the town and its stronghold, Fort Sackville.

Vincennes did not remain too long in American hands, for suddenly in mid-December Colonel Hamilton descended upon the town with 500 whites and Indians and reoccupied its fort. Colonel Clark reacted vigorously. Assembling a force of only 127 men, half of whom were French, he started on an overland march to Vincennes.

Napoleon said that poverty, privation and misery is the school of the soldier. This march in midwinter, sometimes through icy water shoulder deep, certainly proved it. Fortunately Hamilton's Indian allies deserted, leaving him with only 100 men, so after a short resistance he surrendered on February 25, 1779.

The Illinois country remained under American control, although savage fighting continued all along the frontier until the end of the war. Rarely have so few done so much to affect the future of our country. There can be no doubt that their achievement had a great deal to do with the fact that at the peace table the Old Northwest was granted to the United States.

While George Rogers Clark was having such great success two shocking events occurred in Western Pennsylvania and New York. These were the terrible massacres by Indians and whites at Wyoming Valley (Wilkes-Barre, Pennsylvania) in July, and at Cherry Valley (west of Albany) in November, 1778. The punitive expedition

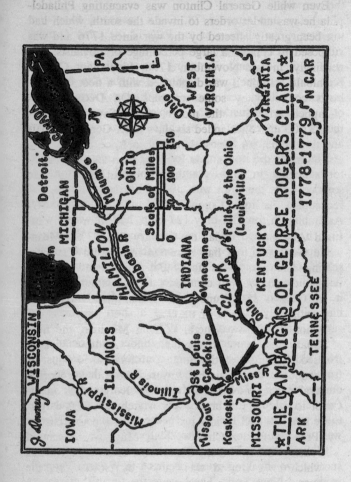

against the Indians would not however take place until the following year.

Even while General Clinton was evacuating Philadelphia he was under orders to invade the south, which had not been greatly affected by the war since 1776 and was supposed to contain a large percentage of Loyalists. Accordingly, in late November, 1778, Lieutenant Colonel Archibald Campbell was dispatched with a fleet of transports convoyed by some warships. On December 23 Campbell arrived at the mouth of the Savannah River with 3,500 men and landed six days later. General Robert Howe marched to oppose him with a force of only 700 Continentals and 150 militia. Against such a small American contingent Campbell easily triumphed and occupied Savannah.

Brigadier General Augustine Prevost, the British commander in East Florida, came north and Campbell captured Augusta, Georgia, on January 29, 1779. Meanwhile General Howe had retreated into South Carolina, leaving Georgia to its fate, and had joined General Benjamin Lincoln who commanded the Southern Department. Georgia passed under almost complete British control until near the end of the war.

Minor actions by General William Moultrie, the hero of Charleston in 1776, and Colonel Andrew Pickens aroused the spirits of the South Carolina patriots just as the conquest of Georgia had aroused those of the Tories. General Lincoln decided to recover Georgia, but an attempt to do so in February and March failed. A larger, more strenuous effort in April resulted in a counterstroke by Prevost toward Charleston in May, which caused Lincoln to withdraw from Georgia. In these engagements, in which little ground was gained by either side, the patriots suffered much heavier losses.

During the summer of 1779 the southern theater saw no actions of consequence except for a British expedition which sacked and burned Portsmouth, Virginia, in

May. But military activity did revive in the north. On June 1 Clinton occupied Stony Point on the west side of the Hudson and Verplanck's Point on the opposite shore, then began enlarging the forts at these points.

From the entire army Washington had created a brigade of light infantry composed of men especially selected from every regiment for agility, alertness and daring. General Wayne, who had earned the name "Mad Anthony" for his vigor and reckless daring in battle, was selected to command this force of about 1,360 men. In it were such steadfast officers as Colonels Christian Febiger and Return Jonathan Meigs who had served with distinction in almost every campaign of the war.

"Mad Anthony" was given the task of taking Stony Point which was occupied by a garrison of over 600 men in a position which was practically immune to attack except by a surprise assault. He decided to advance during the night with bayonets only; not a musket was to be loaded, except in one battalion. Every precaution was taken; selected axemen and special parties led the way. Early in the morning, just after midnight of July 16, he and his brigade rushed and overwhelmed the British garrison. It was a magnificent feat of arms; the fort itself was captured in not much more than half an hour. Although Washington later inspected the fort and decided it was too large to hold, and Clinton later reoccupied it, none of this detracted from the exploit—which proved to all what this new army could do!

On August 19 Major Henry "Light-Horse Harry" Lee conducted a similar attack against Paulus Hook (now a part of Jersey City). It was successful, but not quite as spectacularly so as Wayne's exploit. Two things were accomplished: it kept the British worried about all their outposts, and it brought Lee's name to the attention of the country at large.

In July, 1779, Chief Joseph Brant perpetrated another outrage against the village of Minisink about ten miles

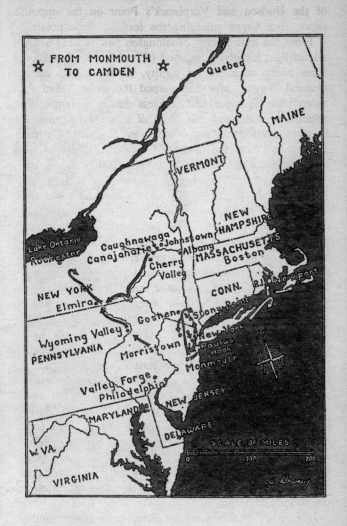

FROM MONMOUTH TO CAMDEN

OHIO
PENNSYLVANIA
MARYLAND
NEW JERSEY
DELAWARE

■ Major British Posts
Established May-Aug, 1780

WEST VIRGINIA

VIRGINIA

Portsmouth

Hillsboro

NORTH CAROLINA

Waxhaws
Great Falls
SOUTH
CAROLINA
Ninety-Six

Cheraw
Camden

Wilmington

Savannah

Augusta

FEB-APR '79

JAN '79

SEP '79

MAY '79

GEORGIA

Savannah

DEC '78

JAN '79

SEP '79

Georgetown

Charleston
FEB-MAY '80

N

FROM MONMOUTH
☆ TO CAMDEN ☆

SCALE OF MILES
0   100   200

FLORIDA

St. Augustine

J. Downey

northwest of Goshen, New York, then defeated and massacred a pursuing force. Within the next few days other small towns in Pennsylvania and New York were destroyed. Meanwhile an expedition was being prepared to punish the Indians and their Tory allies for the massacres at Wyoming Valley and Cherry Valley. It was a double column of 3,700 men including artillery, led by Major General John Sullivan and Brigadier General James Clinton, composed mostly of Continental troops. Directed against the Six Nations, with little regard as to which were friendly and which were not, it inflicted great devastation and destruction but caused few casualties and captured practically no hostages.

As a result of the failure to take hostages, the Tories and Indians, under Sir John Johnson, struck back in May and June of the following year at Caughnawaga and Johnstown, New York. In August Chief Brant destroyed Canajoharie. Thus the war on the frontier of New York continued.

While Sullivan's expedition against the Six Nations was still in progress the seat of war again shifted southward. Upon America's invitation, Admiral Comte d'Estaing sailed from the West Indies where he had repaired after the futile attempt at Newport, and arrived off Savannah with a large fleet and 6,000 soldiers on September 8, 1779.

The British general Prevost started rebuilding the old defenses of the city and erecting additional ones. With the reinforcements which reached him his troops numbered almost 3,200, mostly American Loyalists from the south or some who had previously been brought down from the north. It also included Hessians as well as British.

Pulaski's Legion joined the French troops, a portion of which had been landed on September 12. General Lincoln brought some others, which gave the besiegers about 5,000 men. If these had attacked immediately the city would probably have been taken. But the assault was delayed while the attackers undertook regular siege operations and the defenders were given over two weeks to strengthen their works. When the attack finally did come on October 9 the allies were repulsed with a loss of over 800 men including the gallant Count Casimir Pulaski who was mortally wounded. The defenders lost only 150 men killed, wounded and missing. The result further increased ill feeling between the Americans and the French. Admiral d'Estaing sailed away; Lincoln returned to Charleston.

British losses at sea continued to mount during this period. The destruction of commerce by American privateers was far greater than is generally known and was an important factor in making the continuation of the American war constantly more distasteful to the British public. Also during this period the most spectacular exploit of Captain John Paul Jones' career occurred. Benjamin Franklin, then in Paris, obtained an old French ship which Jones refitted, crowded guns aboard, and renamed the *Bon Homme Richard* in honor of the author of *Poor Richard's Almanac*. With this as his flagship Jones set sail for England with a small squadron. Although some of the French ships deserted him en route and Captain Landais of the American ship *Alliance* proved insubordinate, Captain Jones nevertheless managed to capture a number of prizes.

On the return trip to France the squadron sighted a convoy of merchantmen escorted by the heavily armed frigate *Serapis* and a smaller ship, the *Countess of Scarborough*. Without hesitation, Jones laid his nondescript craft alongside the *Serapis;* the resultant "moonlight battle" fought off Flamborough Head on September 23, 1779, is one of the most famous in naval history. Summoned to surrender, with his ship sinking under him, Jones shouted the memorably defiant answer, "I have not yet begun to fight!"

The *Alliance* was no help; Captain Landais even fired into the *Bon Homme Richard*. But American marksmen in the rigging took a heavy toll on the enemy's deck and a grenade hurled by a marine exploded in the *Serapis'* magazine. When its mainmast fell Captain Richard Pearson struck his flag, and just in time for Jones to transfer his crew—half of whom were casualties—from his blazing ship to the captured enemy. The *Bon Homme Richard* sank the next day.

One of the French ships, the *Pallas,* took the *Countess of Scarborough.* Thereupon Captain Jones brought his ships back to a French port. The moral effect of this victory within sight of the English coast was immense.

That winter of 1779–80 Washington encamped with most of his army at Morristown, New Jersey. The winter at Valley Forge has come to stand for the worst that he and his army had to endure. Generally speaking this is true, but there was still the hunger, the lack of clothing, and for a while the shortage of proper huts. The weather though was worse, with snows piling up to a depth of four feet and the cold much more bitter than at Valley Forge. When spring came the troops were inexpressibly relieved, although it brought bad news from down south.

XIX

The Siege of Charleston

IN the fall of 1779, Newport, Rhode Island, was evacuated, the British force withdrawn and added to the New York garrison. On the day after Christmas, leaving Von Knyphausen to command New York City, General Clinton, with Cornwallis as second in command, sailed southward with 8,500 troops convoyed by Admiral Marriot Arbuthnot.

He landed about thirty miles below Charleston in February, 1780, and advanced slowly upon the city, then called for more men from Savannah and also New York. These came in March and April, giving him a force of about 14,000 including sailors from the fleet.

General Benjamin Lincoln, vastly outnumbered even with reinforcements sent by Washington from Morristown, was forced for political reasons to attempt to defend the city. He surely knew that it was better to save the army and let Charleston go; that the preservation of the fighting force was far more important than the defense of the city. However, the enemy's advance was so slow that he was able to strengthen the harbor defenses of Fort Moultrie on Sullivan's Island and of Fort Johnson on

James Island to the south, which had been allowed to fall into disrepair.

A small canal was dug across the peninsula, a line of fortifications was erected behind it, and a strong redoubt known as the Citadel was built behind this line. Another smaller redoubt was also built on the southeast tip of the peninsula. Finally a log-and-chain boom was erected across the Cooper River, behind which the small American fleet took station. The defense seemed well organized but it was all illusory, as there was no way of escape if Clinton and the British fleet chose to invest it as they could easily do. There was no hope of adequate reinforcement from anywhere. A total of nearly 5,200 Continentals and militia, about equally divided in numbers, awaited capture.

The British moved slowly and stolidly, obviously in no hurry. They did not cross the Ashley River until the end of March. On April 8 Admiral Arbuthnot sent some frigates into Charleston Harbor. Two days later Clinton, having completed his first lines of approach by standard siege methods, called on the city to surrender. The only way left open now was via the Cooper River but no one used it and the summons was refused. Soon that route was closed by Lieutenant Colonel Banastre Tarleton and his British Legion (American Tories) reinforced by Major Patrick Ferguson's American Volunteers and a force of British regulars. Yet the siege went on for nearly a month. Credit is due the defenders who held out so long with no hope at all.

A great deal of the time was spent in attempting to negotiate. In this the military and civilian authorities of Charleston could not agree. Their requests were refused by the enemy in every case; the siege went on.

The Americans attempted a sortie which accomplished little. Admiral Arbuthnot sent a landing force of sailors and marines against Fort Moultrie which surrendered on May 6, thus ending the Revolutionary story of that gal-

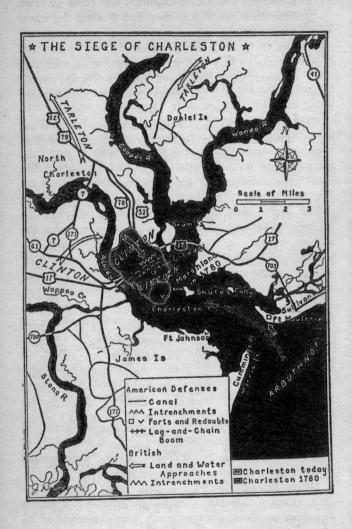

★ THE SIEGE OF CHARLESTON ★

lant outwork which had saved Charleston in the days of 1776. By May 8 the British engineers had come so close to finishing their work that they had drained the canal across the peninsula by a side trench. The final denouement was a bombardment started by the Americans in the evening of May 9 in which every gun on each side fired all night; a terrible night for the citizens whose houses were set on fire. At this point and perhaps because of the ferocious cannonade all agreed to surrender.

On May 12, 1780, the Continental troops marched out to lay down their arms beside the Citadel and become prisoners of war. They had done most of the fighting and suffered most of the casualties. Clinton captured over 390 guns. The militia and the armed citizens of the town were treated as prisoners on parole and allowed to disperse to their homes after also laying down their arms. The Continentals and the militia together gave up nearly 6,000 muskets. They suffered only 240 casualties, a minor amount compared with the loss of so many soldiers by capture. The British gain had been stupendous, over 5,400 individuals captured, with the loss of only 265 men killed and wounded.

Lincoln's surrender of Charleston had been a foregone conclusion. Only the date had been in doubt. It was a major British victory and an American disaster to be compared in this war only with the loss of Fort Washington and the British surrenders at Saratoga and Yorktown. In each of the American disasters the cause had been political. Too much attention had been paid to the wishes of Congress and/or the desires of the local citizens of a great city. In each case two lessons had been learned: the military man on the spot must make the decision based on military considerations; also the retention of a fort or city is not nearly as important as the maintenance of the army in the field, ready to come back and fight again. These lessons have had to be learned time and time again in almost every war.

Now with the American army gone, South Carolina was practically lost to the colonies. Clinton made ready to return to New York, certain that Cornwallis would finish off both of the Carolinas.

XX

The Battle of Camden

THERE was no real campaign leading to the Battle of Camden, although there was some preliminary fighting.

After the fall of Charleston the British established a ring of posts across the northern part of the state, the principal one being at Camden, with others to the north, east and west. These posts were established with ease. The last Continental unit in the state was eliminated on May 29 at the Waxhaws when Lieutenant Colonel Banastre Tarleton with his Tory and British cavalry fell on a body of Virginia cavalry and practically massacred it.

Colonel Tarleton was an able, energetic officer, but quite merciless; not at all a fair sample of the average British officer. At the Waxhaws many men who had surrendered were slaughtered; from this battle came the phrase "Tarleton's quarter," meaning massacre of defenseless men.

In any event the last organized resistance in the state had been eliminated. Clinton left for New York, leaving Cornwallis with about 8,300 men, British and Loyal American troops, to occupy South Carolina and proceed into North Carolina. But this occupation of South Carolina never became a simple affair. It developed into a furious struggle between patriots and Tories, which did not normally involve British regular troops but did involve many of their American allies. It was a true civil war waged in a most violent manner. The three patriotic Americans whose names became best known for keeping alive the spirit of resistance in the south were Francis Marion, Thomas Sumter and Andrew Pickens; all three became brigadier generals. They and their partisans were always active whether with Continental troops or not, whether with large numbers or small, and were a source of confusion to their enemies at all times.

Meanwhile there was a small American Continental force in North Carolina under the command of Major General Baron de Kalb. It consisted of four Maryland regiments commanded by Brigadier General William Smallwood, and three more plus the Delaware regiment under Brigadier General Mordecai Gist, plus Armand's (formerly Pulaski's) Legion. No finer troops could be found in the army than these, but they only numbered 1,400.

Then Congress selected General Horatio Gates, the "hero of Saratoga," to command in the south. The disaster of Charleston was about to be followed by another disaster.

Gates took over command from de Kalb and happily blundered on southward. Against the advice of officers who knew the country, he took the wrong road through deserted areas where supplies could not be found. That march was a nightmare. The men came down with dysentery from eating green corn which was the only food they could find, and were forced to fall out from sheer exhaustion and debilitation. Finally upon reaching greener pastures, Gates was joined by North Carolina and Virginia militia. The difference between the Continentals (even though wasted by the terrible march) and the militia was about to be shown in the most drastic manner.

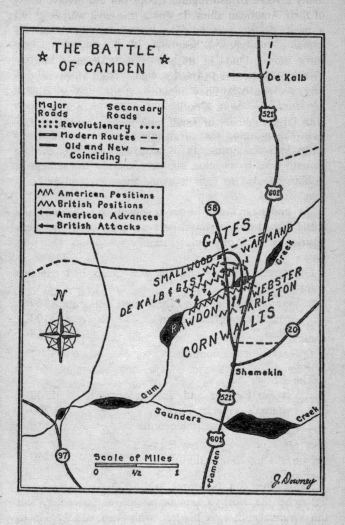

After some preliminary slight maneuvering against Lieutenant Colonel Lord Francis Rawdon in which Gates blundered incredibly, lost two days and weakened his force by a large detachment, he simply issued orders for a night march toward Camden. In the meantime Cornwallis had hastened to the town bringing some reinforcements and had also ordered a night march toward Gates. They met to the surprise of both on the night of August 15–16, 1780. After this meeting engagement they made preparations for the next day's battle.

In the morning the combatants awoke to find themselves in a pine forest, thinly studded with trees, flanked on both sides by swamps, allowing no room for maneuver. If both decided to fight it would mean a head-on collision.

To understand the forces involved and the way the battle turned out, it would be best to set down the composition of each in tabular form.

Of some 4,100 present, the Americans had effective for duty:

Veteran Maryland and Delaware Continentals	900
Armand's Veteran Legion	100
Militia	2050
	3050

The British had:

Veteran Regular and Tory troops	1500
Tarleton's Veteran Cavalry	200
Militia and comparable units	550
	2250

Gates lined up his force with 600 Continentals on the right, the North Carolina militia in the center, and the Virginia militia on his left, with Armand's Legion to their rear. Three hundred Continentals were held in reserve. Thus his strength was on his right or west flank.

Oddly enough Cornwallis did exactly the same, creating an opposite effect. He posted his best men on his right or east flank, with the Highlanders and Tarleton's cavalry in reserve. However, this did not mean that his left was composed of nothing but poor troops, whereas both the American center and left had nothing but poorly trained units who had never seen battle.

The result could have been predicted. In the early morning when the British advanced all along the line and the artillery opened fire enveloping the atmosphere in smoke, the Virginia militia made a halfhearted attempt to stand, then fled. The North Carolina militia, except a single regiment alongside the Continentals, took one look at those murderous British bayonets and ran, scarcely firing a shot. The fleeing militia swept Armand's little Legion from the field. This left 900 Continentals plus one regiment to face 2,250 men.

General Gates was on his horse going away from the battle as fast as he could go. Baron de Kalb and General Gist held the 600 on the American right firm against all assaults by Lord Rawdon's men, even counterattacking. They had not heard from Gates and thought they were winning, which in fact they were on that front.

But now de Kalb called for the reserve and something worse developed. Those 300 had been engulfed by the flying horde of fugitives, then had rallied and tried to come forward. Cornwallis swung his troops against their left flank and against their front. They held firm for a while, rallied, then retreated. That left 600 to face the entire British army.

The valiant 600 fought on and on. Cornwallis launched his full force against them. Still they held on until Tarleton's cavalry hit them in the rear. Baron de Kalb was captured with eleven wounds, dying three days later. The rest kept on until the tide swept over them; a few escaped.

That was the Battle of Camden, the worst defeat ever inflicted upon an American army in battle. The British losses were 324. The American casualties, killed, wounded and missing, were approximately 1,050, of which the Continentals suffered 650, over two-thirds of their number. To this must be added the hundreds of militia who disappeared, presumably fleeing to their homes.

XXI

From Camden to Guilford Court House

AFTER the disastrous American defeat at Camden and General Gates' precipitous flight to Hillsboro, North Carolina (200 miles in three days), the remainder of the Continentals withdrew sullenly, pursued for a distance of twenty miles. Assembled together and led by Generals Smallwood and Gist, this remnant could not catch up to the fleet-footed Gates by marching, until three weeks had passed. Here began the reorganization of the American forces to which a few recruits were added plus a number of soldiers who had survived the defeat at the Waxhaws in May.

The year 1780 was certainly a gloomy one for the patriot cause. The war was definitely being lost in the south, but it was not going well anywhere else for that matter. The past winter had brought the usual trials and tribulations to Washington, made severe this time by the impossible conditions of the currency. If the soldiers were paid at all it was in worthless paper. The phrase "not worth a Continental," applying to the money issued, was worth more than the paper itself.

September, 1780, found the Indians on the warpath again in New York's Mohawk Valley from which they were eventually driven. But the most shocking news of the month was that of Benedict Arnold's treachery at West Point, New York. A great deal has been written pro and con about Arnold's treason. Many have found excuses for him; others denounce him bitterly and without extenuation. The prime factor would seem to be, not so much that he planned to change sides, but that in so doing he sought to deliver to the enemy the important post of West Point with whose defense he had been entrusted.

The tragic figure in this episode is that of Major John André, the adjutant general of Clinton's army. There was great sympathy for him in America, but the court-martial could not possibly have taken any other action than to find him guilty and sentence him to death by hanging. For he had been taken in disguise, with the traitor's papers concealed in his boots. The story of André's flight and near escape has been told and is worth reading for itself alone. The unfortunate part of it for the Americans is that Arnold learned of his capture in time to escape himself.

But with the darkness often comes the dawn. It would come slowly but surely, and the actors were already on the stage. In July, 1780, a small French fleet and an army of 5,000 men commanded by Lieutenant General Comte de Rochambeau had arrived at Newport, Rhode Island. Magnificently attired, disciplined and equipped, they impressed everyone. Furthermore they were to be under Washington's orders. He wanted to use them in an attack on New York. But the small French fleet was soon blockaded in Newport; this ruined the design against New York, and Rochambeau remained idle in Newport to be eventually used in the winning strike at Yorktown.

Two leaders who would bring victory appeared in the south. They were Major General Nathanael Greene, who had been Washington's choice for that command instead of Gates, and Daniel Morgan. The latter affords a striking contrast to Arnold, for Morgan was still a colonel, having been passed over for promotion by many officers who deserved far less of their country. He had resigned in disgust, but after the defeat at Camden had come forth again to fight for his country. Shortly thereafter he was finally promoted.

In the meantime Cornwallis had organized his victorious army and was driving northward into North Carolina. One detachment of his army, led by Major Patrick Ferguson, was operating independently in the mountains to the west, never expecting to find any serious opposition, when suddenly the mountaineers of Virginia, Tennessee and the Carolinas rose against him. Retreating to what he conceived as an impregnable position on King's Mountain, Major Ferguson awaited attack. When it came the British were completely defeated; the American mountaineers, who were all superb sharpshooters, simply stormed up the steep sides and shot down or captured the British defenders. Ferguson was killed. The odd part is that he was the only British participant in the battle; all the others on both sides were Americans, patriots or Tories. This Battle of King's Mountain fought on October 7, 1780, temporarily stopped Cornwallis' northward advance. He felt it necessary to fall back to South Carolina for the protection of its western borders.

This battle provided a great moral stimulus for the Americans. The partisan bands increased in numbers and activity. The little American army which had been collected after Camden advanced to Charlotte. It was still a pitifully small force, but as Greene saw the situation, it should be used somehow to attack whenever possible and also encourage the partisans who were always a thorn in the British side. Here was the beginning of the Greene strategy which eventually won back the complete south.

Before describing the remainder of the war in the southern theater, there are two other events that must be outlined. The first of these was called a "Mutiny,"

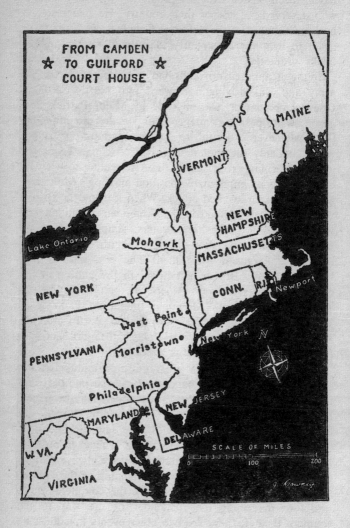

FROM CAMDEN
★ TO GUILFORD ★
COURT HOUSE

MAINE

VERMONT

NEW
HAMPSHIRE

Lake Ontario

Mohawk

MASSACHUSETTS

NEW YORK

CONN.   R.I.
Newport

West Point

New York   N

PENNSYLVANIA

Morristown

Philadelphia

NEW JERSEY

MARYLAND

DELAWARE

W. VA.

SCALE OF MILES

0   100   200

VIRGINIA

J. Downey

OHIO

PENNSYLVANIA   MARYLAND   NEW JERSEY
                                    DELAWARE

Marckes
← Prior to King's Mountain
← From King's Mountain to Cowpens
← From Cowpens to Guilford Court House
WEST VIRGINIA

James Williamsburg
VIRGINIA Yorktown
Richmond

Portsmouth

Guilford Court House   Hillsboro
NORTH   CAROLINA

King's

Cowpens   Charlotte

Cheraw
SOUTH   Waxhaws
CAROLINA   Camden
Ninety-Six

Wilmington

N

Charleston

GEORGIA
Savannah

FROM CAMDEN
☆ TO GUILFORD ☆
COURT HOUSE

SCALE OF MILES
0   100   200

FLORIDA

although in fact it never reached that stage. Many soldiers had been enlisted for "three years or during the war." Naturally this could be construed in either way. On the evening of the first day of January, 1781, the enlisted men of the Pennsylvania Line at Morristown deposed their officers and announced that they would march on Philadelphia. They said that they had been enlisted for three years, while many of their officers had insisted that meant longer if the war lasted over three years. General Wayne showed great courage in going to talk to them in an attempt to bring them back to their duty, but the men insisted on going to see the Congress. It was an unusual mutiny in that they also insisted that they were ready to fight the enemy at any time. It was so obvious that they meant no treason that an agreement was eventually reached which gave them justice in enlistments and pay. There was a later revolt among the New Jersey troops which was easily put down.

The second event occurred in Virginia where, in the same month of January, 1781, Benedict Arnold, now a brigadier general in the British Army, led a venture up the James River. Meeting only negligible resistance, his troops entered Richmond which had been the capital of the colony since 1779. It had been moved from Williamsburg because it was nearer the center of the state and thought to be safer. Arnold destroyed a great deal of property, then returned to Portsmouth.

In the south General Greene split his little army into two parts, which seemed to violate every military maxim. But extraordinary times require extraordinary measures. In order to protect himself from Greene's force (the slightly larger of the two) and from Morgan's force, Cornwallis was forced to divide his army into two, and as it subsequently developed, into three parts. Then he made the mistake of sending Tarleton after Morgan.

XXII

The Battle of Cowpens

WHEN Brigadier General Daniel Morgan turned to face Lieutenant Colonel Banastre Tarleton at the Cowpens he knew there were two active American armies in the Carolinas versus three active British armies. The two American forces were his and Major General Greene's, and they not only were outnumbered by General Lord Cornwallis' three forces, but were also vastly inferior in training, equipment and experience. Furthermore he was well over 100 miles away from Greene by road and had chosen a place from which there was no retreat if defeated.

The numbers engaged in the Battle of Cowpens fought on January 17, 1781, were almost equal—about 1,100 on each side. But in trained regulars Tarleton had about three to Morgan's one and as great a preponderance of cavalry. The field selected was an open woods with trees but no underbrush or swamps and a river to the rear. It seems as if Morgan deliberately picked a place where his men couldn't run or hide and would have to fight. The place was called the Cowpens because it was used as a spot to round up stray cattle; a possible appropriate place for Tarleton to round up all of his enemy after defeating them.

Whatever Daniel Morgan's reasons were for his choice of a battle site, his troop dispositions were superb. He showed an excellent psychological understanding of the capabilities and limitations of his militia, a complete confidence in his Continental infantry which was thoroughly justified, and a superb knowledge of the proper handling of his limited cavalry force. He also predicted exactly how his opponent would fight the battle.

Morgan divided his small army into three parts. The first line, composed entirely of undependable militia, numbered 450 men. His orders to them were completely novel and as unorthodox as was his decision to put them in the first line to receive the initial shock of battle. Some of these were sharpshooters who were placed farther in front, to hide behind trees, fire two volleys, and then join the others. When forced to retreat, the whole 450 were to retire around to the left behind the rest of the Americans.

The second line, also numbering about 450 men, was posted on a low hill overlooking the battlefield. This was the main line composed of Maryland and Delaware Continentals plus some Virginia and Georgia militia, most of whom had previously served an enlistment in the Continental army. The third part of the army, composed of cavalry, was hidden behind another low hill to the rear. All the men were rested, well prepared and ready for the fight.

Tarleton, on the other hand, too eager for the forthcoming battle in which he fully expected to defeat the elusive Americans, awoke his men long before daybreak; without rest he drove them forward so that they arri tired after a long march. Following a hasty personal reconnaissance, Tarleton sent the Legion cavalry at the sharpshooters, who fired from behind their trees and then

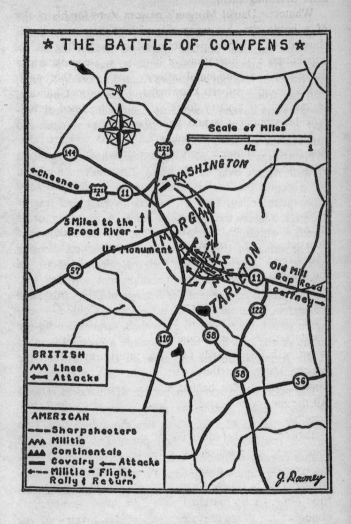

fell back. But this was sufficient to cause the cavalry to lose interest in any further fighting.

Tarleton then formed a standard line of battle with the infantry in the center, fifty dragoons on each wing, and a Highland regiment and the dispirited Legion cavalry in reserve. He promptly opened battle by sending the whole line forward. Morgan's first line reacted as ordered, fired, then ran around to their left. Their successful escape was aided by the cavalry, headed by Lieutenant Colonel William Washington, which swung around the same flank and attacked the advancing British.

Then began the real battle. Somewhat disorganized by their victory over the first line, Tarleton's men rushed at the second line, who received them coolly, firing steadily volley after volley. Tarleton moved his Highland reserve regiment against the American right. A mistaken order caused a withdrawal but Morgan and his officers checked it. The crisis of the battle had been reached. Sensing victory, the British rushed forward. Facing about, in one blinding crash, the Continentals sent a volley into the disordered enemy ranks at a range of fifty yards, then charged with the bayonet. Simultaneously Colonel Washington struck them, and to everyone's surprise so did the militia of the first line, who had made a complete circuit of the American forces and now hit the British on the flank.

The main battle was over but the Highlanders refused to recognize it, fighting on grimly, much as the Continentals had at Camden. The British artillerymen, true to their tradition, died at their posts. The disheartened Legion cavalry refused to take part and fled. In the pursuit Washington caught up with Tarleton. Although neither was hurt, the most famous picture of the battle depicts this encounter.

The victory was decisive and complete. Of the 1,100 British engaged, 930 were killed, wounded or captured, while of an almost equal number engaged, the Americans lost only 70 killed and wounded.

Yet in spite of his splendid victory Morgan was not out of danger. Cornwallis still had two armies left which were larger than Greene's and Morgan's. Furthermore Cornwallis was in the process of uniting his two and placing them between the American forces. Morgan must move fast to escape this threat, yet he was encumbered with his and the British captured wounded plus all his prisoners.

Fortunately Cornwallis, although normally aggressive, waited until it was too late and then moved in the wrong direction to catch the fast-moving Americans. Cornwallis did destroy all his superfluous baggage but lost precious time in doing it. So Morgan escaped, after his decisive victory, to eventually rejoin Greene. The subsequent events properly belong in the account of Guilford Court House in which Morgan did not take part. Suffering from ague and rheumatism, he retired and returned to his home in Virginia. No one could have felt more satisfied with his last battle for his country. It had been superb; one of the few perfectly fought classic victories in military history.

XXIII

The Battle of Guilford Court House

GENERAL Greene knew that of the two parts of his army the one that was in the most precarious position was Morgan's, since it had to follow a circuitous route to join. Greene therefore left the other division under the command of Brigadier General Isaac Huger to march from Cheraw northward while he went with a couple of aides to meet Morgan. Together they escaped Cornwallis' troops and joined Huger at Guilford Court House so that Greene had a chance to look over the ground long before the battle was fought.

The greater fame of Washington's retreat to Trenton and Princeton, has tended to obscure the events of Greene's retreat through North Carolina to Virginia and his subsequent return to Guilford Court House. The two are comparable both in the privations endured and the subsequent results. Yet Greene's was a planned retreat, designed to lure Cornwallis away from his base of supplies and closer to Virginia where the Americans could expect a few more troops, supplies and equipment. Greene had only 2,000 troops versus 3,000; therefore he could not afford to get caught. The problem was to keep Cornwallis in expectation of being able to do just that, yet barely keep out of his reach.

Greene organized a light corps of troops to keep themselves always interposed between him and the enemy. With Morgan physically unable to continue, Colonel Otho H. Williams was chosen to command this body of troops. And an excellent choice it was. Williams was a tall man, energetic and highly valued by all who knew him. He promptly set to work to organize his men and never once failed in his duty of preventing Cornwallis from reaching the main body, although sometimes it was touch and go because the British led by Brigadier General Charles O'Hara pursued vigorously. The weather was miserable with almost continuous snow and rain. The wonder is that either army managed to make the march. At times it must have seemed beyond the limit of human endurance.

If Cornwallis should win the race the war in the south would be practically over. Fortunately Greene had made provision ahead of time for boats to be collected at the river crossing sites, while the British had to march by the upper fords. These preparatory measures and Colonel Williams' light corps undoubtedly saved the chase for the Americans. Finally in mid-February, 1781, the last of the troops got over the last river into Virginia after marching forty miles in sixteen hours.

Now the aggressive Cornwallis had gone too far. He had chased the only organized American force out of the Carolinas, but the minute his army went farther northward into Virginia, Greene would be reinforced by Von Steuben who had been collecting a force of Continentals in that colony. The British would then be outnumbered. The only sensible thing for them to do now was to retreat to the south. Their base was over 200 miles away. In an effort to march faster Cornwallis had destroyed a great portion of his army's supplies and now he could get nothing from the countryside. So he returned to Hillsboro,

North Carolina; all his efforts and those of his troops
had been in vain.

Greene's problem was almost as serious. He had retreated a long way safely, but now the problem was to
come back and win a battle. He did not want to retreat
any farther than necessary to be reinforced. He sent Otho
Williams and his light troops, together with "Light-Horse
Harry" Lee's Legion, to harass Cornwallis who then retreated a long way safely, but now the problem was to
maneuvers followed during which Greene was finally reinforced. He then selected Guilford Court House, which
he had surveyed weeks before during the retreat, as a
suitable place to give battle.

On March 15, 1781, the American army consisted
of the following:

1,600	regular Continental infantry
2,200	militia
400	riflemen
220	cavalry and artillery
4,420	Total

This was considerably larger than the British army
which numbered about 1,900. But less than one half
of the Continentals had been in battle before, and there
was no telling what the others might do. Actually it would
be difficult to predict the outcome of such a battle, but
it was Greene's best chance—to fight now. The time of
service of his riflemen could expire at any time they
chose, and he would be bound to lose others by normal
attrition.

The position chosen by Greene faced west and was
slightly over a mile wide. Through it ran a road which
formed the axis of communications for both armies. There
were two hilly positions on the battlefield. The largest

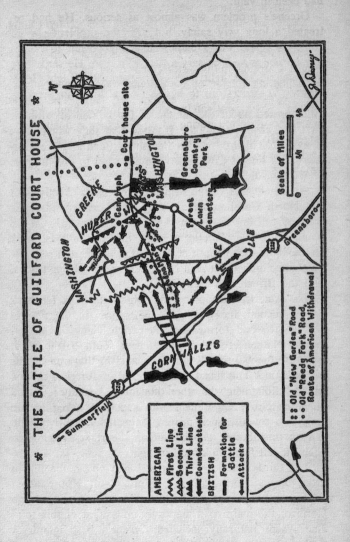

* THE BATTLE OF GUILFORD COURT HOUSE *

N

Scale of Miles

Court house site

GREENE

HUGER

Gen. Greene

WASHINGTON

WASHINGTON

Greensboro
Country
Park

Forest
Lawn
Cemetery

LEE

Greensboro

CORNWALLIS

Summerfield

AMERICAN
▲▲▲ First Line
▲▲▲ Second Line
▲▲▲ Third Line
⬇ Counterattacks
BRITISH
── Formation for
     Battle
➤ Attacks

:: Old "New Garden" Road
·· Old "Reedy Fork" Road,
     Route of American Withdrawal

and steepest was to the southwest. The next hill, on which the court house stood, was to the northeast.

Except for three clearings the area was gently rolling country and well wooded. General Greene formed his troops into three lines. The first was composed of the North Carolina militia with riflemen on each flank plus Washington's Legion on the extreme right, or north flank, and Lee's Legion on the extreme left flank. The militia were posted about the middle of the battlefield with the first two clearings to their front so that they would have a good field of fire for their first shots. For they, like Morgan's first line at Cowpens, were expected to fire just two shots, then fall back.

At the advance of the British center this is exactly what the North Carolina militia did. Their two rounds took a heavy toll but the enemy kept bravely forward. On the south flank the Americans were forced southeast back to the high ground south of the battlefield where a separate combat continued between Lee's Legion, supporting troops, and the British and Hessians.

The American troops on the right north flank fell back to the second line which was 350 yards to the rear in the woods, and formed on their right flank. (The imposing Nathanael Greene Monument south of the road, opposite the Visitor Center, is located in the area of this second line.) This line was made up of the Virginia militia, about 1,200 men who were thought to be better trained than the North Carolinians who had been asked to fire only two rounds. Such proved to be the case; they held a long time before giving way on the right flank. Even then the left flank continued its fight.

The third American line was drawn up on the hill in front of and northwest of Guilford Court House about 350 yards behind the second line. (The tall white cenotaph north of the main road marks the mid-point of this third line which naturally included Greene's best infantry.) Seeing the oncoming British breaking through the right half of the second line, they held their fire until the enemy was within 100 feet, loosed a volley, and drove them with the bayonets across a ravine and up an adjacent slope where they eventually rallied. It is possible that Greene here missed his chance to destroy Cornwallis' army before these troops rallied and while the remainder were still struggling with the left of the second line. On the other hand, if a counterattack failed the army would be gone; the last organized force in the south, the only hope for independence of the southern colonies. So Greene withheld his hand.

Then came the most dramatic phase of the battle. Disengaging themselves from the left half of the second line which was weakening fast, the British plunged forward in force against the third line. When attacked, the Americans on the left of this line gave way in flight. Colonel Washington saw this and drove his horsemen forward into the midst of the enemy. Prominent in this attack was the giant 6-foot-8-inch Peter Francisco, physically the strongest man in either the American or British armies. His exploits have become a part of Virginia history and legend. In this battle he is reputed to have killed eleven men with his huge 5-foot sword.

Simultaneously the next regiment in line, the 1st Maryland Continentals and the Delaware Continental infantry, wheeled and struck the attacking British in flank. The fighting was severe as both sides stood their ground. Into the midst of this confused, desperate melee, Cornwallis ordered his gunners to fire grapeshot. The result was disastrous to both sides. He has been criticized severely for firing into his own British troops as well as those of the enemy, but it was probably the only remedy which permitted the British to reform.

The first British troops again ready for action were those on the slope across the ravine. They charged the Americans but were as fiercely met, then thrown back. Finally there came a pause during which Greene decided to withdraw. Technically Cornwallis had won the battle because he held the field. But his losses had been terrific—over a fourth of his command, more than 530 men killed and wounded.

The American losses can only be stated in killed and wounded, about 260 men. There can be no way of estimating accurately how many ran away or how many of these were wounded. We know that over 1,000 ran away, probably many more. On the other hand Greene was satisfied; his next move was to follow Cornwallis who retreated and ultimately left the Carolinas to go to Virginia and Yorktown.

XXIV

From Guilford Court House
to Yorktown

LEAVING the campaign to recover the south to a separate chapter, we revert to the New York frontier. In January the Indians had again struck, and in May, Fort Stanwix, the key post at the entrance to the Mohawk Valley which had been damaged by floods and partially destroyed by fire, was abandoned. Colonel Marinus Willett undertook to drive the Indians out of the lower Mohawk Valley, which he accomplished in the early part of July 1781. The upper part of the valley was not finally cleared until the latter part of October; the news from Yorktown may have had something to do with the end of the Indian depredations.

Washington, in New York, must have thought a great deal about his native state of Virginia which was now for the first time feeling the impact of the war. He must have particularly resented the fact that it was the traitor Benedict Arnold who was leading the enemy force there. Of course Washington never took his eyes off the largest enemy target of New York City, but he did devise a scheme to bring help to Virginia.

Lafayette was dispatched there with 1,200 seasoned Continentals. This was not a large enough force to combat

Arnold's 1,600 men, but with his thoughts always concerned with the command of the sea, Washington also arranged for the French fleet to convoy 1,200 additional French troops. Unfortunately, owing to the arrival of a British fleet, this venture was defeated. Then General Clinton sent Major General William Phillips with 2,600 more British troops.

The enemy operations in Virginia began in earnest. In April, 1781, Arnold, with a large force, captured Petersburg, which was defended only by a small body of militia. Both Phillips and Arnold continued to operate in that vicinity, destroying quantities of supplies and several vessels. Late in the month Lafayette arrived at Richmond and was soon reinforced by militia to a strength of 3,000 men. This did little good, for Cornwallis arrived in Virginia with 1,500 men. A reinforcement of 1,500 more came from Clinton, bringing the total British strength to 7,200 men. Cornwallis promised to soon take care of Lafayette and his small army; he is reputed to have referred contemptuously to Lafayette as "the boy."

"The boy" proved thoroughly competent. He had learned his lesson well from Washington and from reading of Greene's campaigns. Late in May, Cornwallis moved north, by-passing Richmond, but could not catch Lafayette who kept him occupied with a series of skirmishes but avoided any possibility of a real battle. And Lafayette was expecting a reinforcement from Washington led by General Wayne, which he must meet without interference from his enemy. He conducted a series of rapid marches northward to near Fredericksburg where they joined.

Cornwallis meanwhile gave up trying to catch his elusive foe and sent Tarleton on a wild-goose chase to Charlottesville where the legislature was now in session. A swift-riding horseman named Captain John Jouett carried the word ahead of him. Thomas Jefferson escaped to the mountains but some others of the legislature were captured. Tarleton did find some supplies en route and in

FROM GUILFORD
COURT HOUSE
TO YORKTOWN

SCALE OF MILES
0   100   200

the town, which he destroyed. That Cornwallis would undertake such schemes as this is indicative of how thoroughly he had, for the present, given up ideas of destroying "the boy" and his army. His forces still far outnumbered Lafayette's but he could not bring the Frenchman to bay. Shortly thereafter he moved back southward to Richmond, entering the town on June 16. The Americans took this as a further confession of his inability to continue the war northward, and in truth it was almost his last step toward the final denouement at Yorktown, although neither he nor his opponents could yet visualize this as the end of the road.

At this time Lafayette, reinforced by Wayne, Steuben's Continentals and militia, still could number only 4,500 men in his force, versus Cornwallis' 7,200 men. The only thing he could do was follow at a distance and be guided by the moves of his enemy, who unaccountably turned eastward to Williamsburg. The truth is that Cornwallis was beset by conflicting orders from Clinton and Lord Germain, the colonial secretary. Germain believed in the Virginia campaign; Clinton did not, but was also afraid of an attack by Washington and Rochambeau on New York. Distances were immense, and it seemed best to Cornwallis to move toward the east coast where dispatches could reach him sooner. In fact Clinton called for 3,000 men from Cornwallis, so another move was set in progress across the James to Portsmouth where they were to be embarked.

Here Lafayette made his first mistake and almost walked into a trap from which Wayne, by quick presence of mind and sheer bravery, saved the army. The idea was to destroy part of the British army while it was in the process of crossing the river. Lafayette thought he saw his chance on July 6, near Greenspring. Thinking that most of the British were already across the river, he sent Wayne through a deep morass to attack the rear guard, then reinforced him to a strength of 900 men, holding everybody but the militia near at hand to exploit the action. Cornwallis however, expecting just such a move, had almost his entire army on hand, screened only by a small force. Then at the right moment the British general loosed his entire strength. Seeing the oncoming troops, Wayne took the only possible action which could save his force and the American army. He counterattacked with such vigor that he temporarily threw the enemy off balance, then fought a slow, retiring action. The coming of darkness saved the Americans.

After this action Cornwallis did cross the James, sent the 3,000 troops to Portsmouth, and raided the surrounding country. Upon receipt of orders from Clinton telling him to keep all his troops, Cornwallis recrossed the James and established himself at Yorktown. He also seized Gloucester across the York River so that the fleet would have a suitable harbor, protected on both sides.

Up north in late May while Cornwallis was preparing to chase Lafayette out of Richmond, Washington received word that Admiral Comte de Grasse was leaving the West Indies and then coming to the colonies. Preoccupied with thoughts of New York City and recognizing the vital importance of control of the seas in this war, Washington planned an attack on General Clinton. Truly the northern army needed some activity or it would die of inaction. Except for the continuous small skirmishes which were always occurring in the "Neutral Ground" between New York City and Peekskill, there had been nothing taking place for a long time. Also Rochambeau's French army had been lying idle at Newport for almost a year.

Rochambeau agreed to march to the Hudson which he reached early in July. Then came electrifying news. On August 14 a letter from Admiral de Grasse notified Rochambeau and Washington that the French fleet with 3,000 troops aboard was sailing from Santo Domingo to the Chesapeake. This required immediate action and a fateful decision. If Washington went to Yorktown the

Hudson Highlands would be left practically unguarded.
If Clinton advanced up the Hudson he might at one stroke
gain all that the British had striven for in 1776 and 1777
—seize the Hudson River and separate New England from
the rest of the colonies. Yet Washington's hand was
forced; he had to take his long-sought seapower where he
could find it, and the 3,000 French troops could not be
ignored. The audacity and skill of a great leader seized
the occasion, risking all on the endeavor.

General Heath was left to hold the Hudson Highlands
with less than 2,500 men while Washington marched
southward with the rest of the American troops and the
French army. In order to deceive Clinton in New York,
the move was made with the greatest secrecy; an attempt
was also made to make it appear as if an attack might be
launched against New York City from New Jersey. By the
time Clinton learned the truth the allied armies were
passing through Philadelphia.

On September 5 a British fleet commanded by Ad-
mirals Thomas Graves and Samuel Hood appeared off the
Yorktown Capes. They had 19 ships of the line and
were expecting to meet a smaller force. Admiral de Grasse,
who had already landed his 3,000 troops, weighed anchor
and sailed out to give battle. He had 24 ships of the
line and was under the great disadvantage of having to
beat to windward. Admiral Graves, the senior British
officer afloat, handled his ships very poorly and the result
was a conclusive French victory. Additional French warships arrived four days later. Cornwallis was now firmly
bottled up in Yorktown with no escape by sea.

On September 6 General Clinton sent General Arnold,
who had returned to New York in June, on a raid to
New London, Connecticut. The hope was that Washington's attention would be diverted to that quarter and that
this might cause him to send part of his army back toward
New York. The raid turned into a wanton massacre of
soldiers who had surrendered and a useless destruction

of buildings, but failed in its purpose. Washington's armies continued south, refusing to be diverted from their prime purpose by any minor actions no matter how ruthless. On September 26 the forces to besiege Yorktown were all assembled at Williamsburg.

XXV

The Campaign to Recover the South

THE campaign waged by Major General Nathanael Greene after the Battle of Guilford Court House was one of the most unusual ever recorded in American history. It is extremely doubtful if any other general in the Revolution could have been as successful. In our military history it ranks with Stonewall Jackson's Valley Campaign of 1862.

His name will always be linked inseparably with the names of Brigadier Generals Francis Marion, Andrew Pickens and Thomas Sumter, because without them the campaign could never have been won. For Greene was the first general in this war to make skillful, intelligent and combined use of regular and irregular troops.

After the Battle of Guilford Court House, Cornwallis discovered that, although he had won a tactical victory his losses had been so high that he could not afford to risk another battle in an unfriendly country. His supplies were so short and his transportation so scanty that when he left the field he had to leave several of his wounded in Greene's care. He moved to Wilmington, North Carolina, then decided to abandon the Carolinas, leaving them to the care of Lord Rawdon, and enter Virginia.

Greene pursued for a short distance, then swung south.

The enemy had a chain of outposts to be seized in South Carolina and Georgia before those states could be restored to the colonies. Greene knew that his own army was too small to accomplish this by itself. He must use the irregular partisans to help him. The basic plan which he conceived was to use them to harass the enemy's supply lines, seize their smaller bases—if only temporarily—and interrupt their communications so that they could not cooperate effectively while he moved against their separated larger garrisons with his main army. Above all he must preserve his main army intact. He could fight battles against the enemy's major forces but never to the point where—like Cornwallis—he lost so many men that he could not return to fight again. Far better to lose a battle tactically than to push it to a success and then not still be there as the nucleus around which the whole effort to recover the south must be based. For that project could never be accomplished without his army always ready and always in being.

The first thing Greene did was to contact "The Swamp Fox," Francis Marion, send him "Light-Horse Harry" Lee and his Legion, and ask him to take Fort Watson while Greene moved against Lord Rawdon at Camden. Marion took Fort Watson by the ingenious device of erecting a tower of logs outside the walls, higher than the stockade, from which his riflemen shot everything that moved; the garrison surrendered.

Lord Rawdon began the Battle of Hobkirk's Hill, fought a mile and a half north of Camden on April 25, by attacking the American outposts. The result was a sharp engagement in which Greene gave as good as he got but was forced from the field. However Rawdon, like Cornwallis, could not stay where he was and retreated, burning Camden. Thus the British lost one of their major outposts in the northern part of the chain.

Other posts fell with amazing rapidity: Fort Motte, taken by Marion and Lee; Orangeburg, by Sumter; Fort

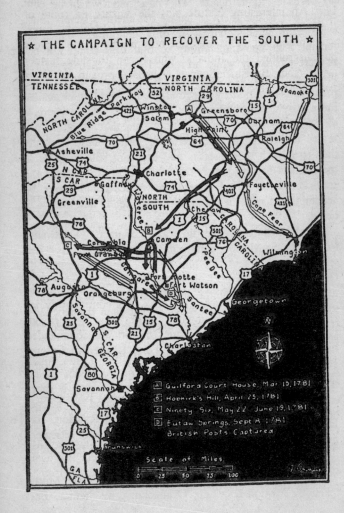

Granby (later the site of Columbia), by Lee; and Georgetown, by Marion. Of all the larger posts in the south, not counting Charleston and Savannah, this left only Ninety-Six in South Carolina and Augusta in Georgia.

Of these Augusta was captured next by Pickens and Lee. An interesting feature was the seizure en route of the annual Crown gift to the Indians of blankets, arms, ammunition, etc. This was not only useful to the captors but disgruntled the Indians, who began to slide further away from British influence. Augusta proved to be a particularly difficult assignment and did not capitulate until June 6 after a siege of two weeks' duration.

Greene himself had not been inactive. While exercising general direction of the operations his eyes had been directed toward the main target, Ninety-Six. When Fort Granby fell he marched. Upon arrival he found that the stockade was far too strong to be taken by assault by the small force at his disposal, so began regular siege operations. These were conducted energetically night and day under the supervision of that able engineer Thaddeus Kosciusko.

On June 8 Lee and his Legion arrived to help. Pickens came soon after and work was begun on the other side of the stockade on another series of parallels designed to cut off the water supply. The work was continuously interrupted by a series of nightly sorties from the garrison. Unfortunately for the Americans, the fort was commanded by an extremely able New York Tory, Lieutenant Colonel John H. Cruger, who conducted one of the most brilliant defensive operations of the entire war.

Unfortunately also, word came that Lord Rawdon was on the way with reinforcements which had come from England. A last desperate assault against the fort was made. When it failed, Greene and his men sullenly withdrew; again he and his army had been defeated. But again the Americans had won. Rawdon ordered the garrison to evacuate the fort, and demolished it.

During the remainder of the month of June and early July the two armies marched and countermarched against each other, feinting and sparring, encountering incredible hardships. Heat and malaria finally forced them both to call a halt for rest and recuperation. Lord Rawdon, his health shattered, left for England; his ship was seized by Admiral Comte de Grasse and he was sent as a prisoner to France. The command was assumed by Lieutenant Colonel Alexander Stuart.

Late in August Greene moved toward Stuart who was encamped near Orangeburg. The rivers were so swollen by the summer rains that Greene was forced to make a wide circuit up the Wateree to Camden, then down the west bank to cross the Congaree where he discovered that Stuart had moved to Eutaw Springs. Greene followed and prepared to fight. A list of the commanders engaged in this last battle sounds almost like a roll call of all the great names of the campaign. On the American side there were Generals Marion, Pickens and Sumter, and Colonels Lee and William Washington, while on the British side there were Colonel Stuart and the redoubtable Colonel Cruger of Ninety-Six fame.

The numbers on September 8, 1781, were about equal: 2,300 Americans versus 2,000 British. Greene attacked and after a particularly obstinate and bloody battle relinquished the field, but both sides were exhausted and each claimed the victory. The Americans lost about 25 per cent of their strength on this day while the British loss was 40 per cent. Then Stuart returned to the vicinity of Charleston.

For all practical purposes the Battle of Eutaw Springs ended the campaign. Except for Charleston and Savannah, South Carolina and Georgia had been regained.

XXVI

The Siege of Yorktown

ON September 26, 1781, when Washington had assembled all his forces for the siege of Yorktown and Gloucester, the allied armies numbered about 16,650 men. Of these nearly 8,850 were Americans and 7,800 were French. However, the French army was undoubtedly the more powerful of the two since all the troops were regulars, thoroughly trained, disciplined and equipped, while 3,000 of the Americans were militia, some of whom had received no previous training.

The American Continental troops were organized into three divisions of two brigades each commanded by Major Generals Lafayette, Lincoln (who had been exchanged after his capture at Charleston) and Von Steuben. The militia was commanded by General Thomas Nelson, Governor of Virginia and a native of Yorktown. The American wing was under the command of General Lincoln, but Washington—while commander in chief of both armies —continued to issue daily orders to the Americans as usual. The French wing of the allied armies was commanded by Lieutenant General Comte de Rochambeau and consisted of seven regiments organized into three brigades.

To defend Yorktown and Gloucester, Cornwallis had an army of only about 7,400 men. Of these about 2,000 were German troops. The British portion was organized into two brigades plus a small brigade of Guards commanded by Brigadier General O'Hara, the only other general officer on the British side, and some light infantry.

Included within the above totals each army had, in addition to the infantry organized as described, its own complements of engineers, cavalry and artillery. The American artillery brigade was commanded by Brigadier General Henry Knox.

Yorktown occupied the center of the stage from the beginning. There was no active siege of Gloucester which was defended by a line of entrenchments drawn across the Point, and initially by a force of 700 infantry and cavalry later strengthened by a few additional cavalry. To contain this force, to check foraging expeditions being conducted from Gloucester Point, and to close a possible avenue of escape for the British army, Washington stationed there a force of 1,500 militia and 600 French infantry and cavalry. A few days later 800 marines from the French fleet were added to the allied forces encircling the Point. Only one skirmish occurred here when on October 3 a foraging party was driven back into the British lines. Thereafter the allies established their camps closer to those of the enemy and held their positions until the end of the siege, the British staying within their lines.

When he occupied Yorktown, Cornwallis' original purpose had been to obtain a good seaport and harbor. He had never envisioned the possibility of having to defend it against a siege from the landward side; it possessed no commanding features overlooking the surrounding terrain. An inner defense line of earthworks, redoubts and batteries was constructed around the town with two redoubts, Numbers 9 and 10, in advance of and as an additional strength to the eastward end of the line.

In the rear of the town there are two ravines which

helped give some protection against an attack. One of these, Yorktown Creek, flowed around the inner defenses to the north, thence into the York River. The other, Wormley Creek, flowed into the river to the east. Beyond the inner defense line a series of outworks was also constructed on both sides of Wormley Creek in the gap beyond the head of the two ravines and northwest of Yorktown near the river. This last was a star-shaped redoubt known as the Fusiliers' Redoubt because it was manned by a portion of the Royal Welch Fusiliers. In addition in the river near the town were some large transports and two frigates, the *Charon* and the *Guadeloupe,* but these had been stripped of a good deal of their armament for use in land defenses.

On September 27 Washington issued his marching orders to the troops who moved out the next day and occupied a line encircling Yorktown within a mile of the British outworks. In doing so they encountered no opposition until close to Yorktown where they met a few enemy pickets who retired about sunset. There were no casualties.

On the following day, September 29, the American wing which was on the right or east side of the encircling line moved farther to its right and nearer the enemy. The entire allied army now spread out into permanent camps that extended in a great curve six miles long from the York River, northwest of the town, around to the south through woods and fields, then east to Wormley Creek. The American wing on the right and the French wing on the left were divided about the middle of the line by the swamps and marshes of Beaverdam Creek.

On the morning of September 30 the allies awoke to a pleasant surprise. During the night Cornwallis had evacuated all of his outworks except the Fusiliers' Redoubt northwest of Yorktown and Redoubts 9 and 10 close to the river on the east side of the town. This was a mistake; any army undergoing a siege should play for time in the hope of obtaining relief, or by occupying the attentions of a large portion of the enemy's troops, influence the action favorably in another locality. As a matter of fact Cornwallis had received information from Clinton the day before that a large fleet and 5,000 men were being readied and would sail to relieve him within a few days. Cornwallis therefore decided that since he need only hold out for a few days it would be easier to do so by occupying only the inner defense line. He should have known that delays inevitably occur in war, and he should never have given up the outworks without a struggle. Clinton's fleet and relieving army actually sailed from New York on the day of the surrender.

Promptly taking advantage of Cornwallis' premature retreat, the Americans and French occupied the abandoned works and immediately began additional construction including a new redoubt. On the left the French advanced against the Fusiliers' Redoubt and drove in the pickets but the position itself was too strongly defended. Although the abandoned outworks and the new construction were subjected to a heavy and sustained fire from the British guns in the main fortifications, the work continued and was completed in about four days.

Meanwhile the real preparations for the siege had begun. During the first days of October the allies completed their surveying and planning, collected and constructed their siege material, and brought up the heavy guns which had been landed at the James River, six miles to the southwest. On the night of October 6–7 while the French made a diversionary attack against the Fusiliers' Redoubt 4,300 men paraded at dusk and marched out between the lines to begin the construction of the first parallel. This was a line of fortifications about 2,000 yards long approximately parallel to the British inner defense line. Its average distance from the main British works was only 800 yards except on the right opposite Redoubts 9 and 10 where the distance was necessarily greater. At this range the allied artillery could easily be brought to bear on the defenders. With 1,500 men at work with the digging while 2,800 men guarded them, the trenches were dug sufficiently deep by morning to protect the men at work on the next day.

The Americans occupied the right half of this new siege line with the French on their left. No attempt was made to extend it farther to the left because of the ravine of Yorktown Creek, although the French did construct a small section opposite the Fusiliers' Redoubt from which guns could be fired against the British ships anchored in the harbor.

For the next two days and nights the work of digging entrenchments, batteries and redoubts in the first parallel was continued at a rapid rate in spite of the gunfire of the British artillery. This formal siege warfare was a novel experience to the American soldiers, completely different from anything they had ever before encountered, but by October 9 the besiegers' artillery was ready. The first to fire was the French battery on the left opposite the Fusiliers' Redoubt; it drove the frigate *Guadeloupe* across the river to the Gloucester shore. Two hours later an American battery joined in the bombardment, General Washington firing the first round. On October 10 the Grand French Battery and another American battery began firing; fifty-two guns were now in action; the superior French and American artillery nearly silenced the British guns. The frigate *Charon* was set on fire and destroyed by red-hot shot from the French battery on the left. The bombardment was so effective that Washington was soon ready to begin the second parallel closer to the British line.

On the night of October 11–12 work began on the second line about midway between the first parallel and the British. About 750 yards were completed that night. For the next three days the construction continued, and although artillery was moved forward from the first parallel, the new line could not be completed on the right.

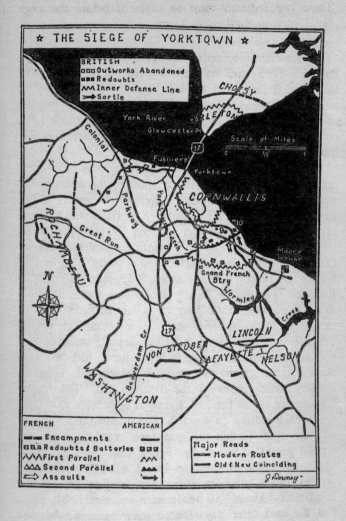

The two British redoubts, Numbers 9 and 10, occupied the ground between the second parallel and the river. These two redoubts must be captured before the siege could progress further.

The last infantry assault of the war was launched on the night of October 14. In a spirit of rivalry the French were assigned Redoubt Number 9 and the Americans Number 10. Each attacking force was composed of 400 men; the French were commanded by Colonel Guillaume de Deux Ponts, the Americans by Lieutenant Colonel Alexander Hamilton. The French target was the stronger of the two forts. It was defended by 120 British and Hessians, while the American target was held by 70 men. Both columns started their assault at eight o'clock in the evening. The Americans stormed Redoubt Number 10 and overcame all resistance in the short space of ten minutes, while the French encountered some difficulties but completed their task in less than half an hour.

Immediately following the capture of these two key redoubts fatigue parties resumed work and by morning had incorporated both into the second parallel. On the following night Cornwallis attempted a sortie near the center of the line. It was a gallant effort, launched just before daybreak of the 16th by 350 men. A few guns were spiked but the assault was repulsed, and soon the disabled guns were again firing on Yorktown.

Cornwallis' situation was now hopeless but he might be able to get some of his troops across the river, break through the Gloucester lines, and escape to New York. Before midnight of October 16 he embarked a number of his men in small boats and landed them on the opposite shore. Then a violent storm arose and scattered the boats, preventing any possibility of a second trip across. The next morning he recalled those who had made the effort.

So at ten o'clock on that same morning, October 17— the fourth anniversary of Burgoyne's surrender—a red-coated drummer mounted the parapet and began to beat a "parley." It is doubtful if anyone could hear him in the midst of the bombardment, but the message was understood. The guns ceased fire; a British officer appeared, was blindfolded and taken into the American lines where he asked for an armistice. Commissioners met at the Moore House on the next day and settled the surrender terms.

At 2:00 P.M. on October 19, 1781, the defeated army marched out from Yorktown clad in a new issue of uniforms, with their colors cased and their bands playing an old British march entitled "The World Turned Upside Down." Cornwallis did not surrender in person; he pleaded illness. The troops were led by Brigadier General Charles O'Hara of the British Guards.

The allies were drawn up in two lines—the French on one side, the Americans on the other. The defeated army marched between these lines. General O'Hara tried first to give Cornwallis' sword to General Rochambeau who motioned him toward Washington. The commander in chief indicated that General Lincoln, who had surrendered to the British under similar circumstances at Charleston, should be handed the sword. O'Hara offered it to Lincoln who accepted the token of surrender and then returned it. The troops marched to the surrender field where they laid down their arms.

Across the river Lieutenant Colonel Tarleton surrendered the troops in the Gloucester lines. Before doing so he told the allied commander, Brigadier General de Choisy, that because of his evil reputation he feared for his life if left in the hands of the militia. De Choisy therefore excluded some of the militia from this surrender ceremony, and everything proceeded smoothly.

A total of 7,247 officers and soldiers and 840 seamen surrendered at Yorktown and Gloucester. The casualties incurred during the siege were fewer than expected. The Americans lost only 20 killed and 56 wounded, the French 52 killed and 134 wounded. The British and Hessian losses were naturally greater, a total of 156 killed and 326 wounded.

This surrender virtually ended the war in America, although some fighting continued on the Ohio frontier, in South Carolina and Georgia. The King was of a mind to continue the war but the British people were overwhelmingly opposed. The ministry fell; a new cabinet was appointed. General Sir Guy Carleton superseded Clinton in the spring of 1782, and shortly after assuming the command in New York wrote Washington asking for a cessation of hostilities. The treaty of peace acknowledging the independence of the United States of America was formally ratified on September 3, 1783.

Bibliography

Of the many books consulted in the preparation of this work, only a few are listed below. They are the ones which furnished the bulk of the information, although to ensure accuracy insofar as possible, the historical data was cross-checked against numerous other primary and secondary sources. Special mention should be made of Christopher Ward's fine military history, *The War of the Revolution*, and *The West Point Atlas of American Wars* which were particularly valuable.

Bill, Alfred H., *Valley Forge, The Making of an Army*. New York: Harper & Brothers, 1952.

Bliven, Bruce Jr., *Battle for Manhattan*. New York: Henry Holt & Co., 1955.

Bowen, Catherine D., *John Adams and the American Revolution*. Boston: Little, Brown & Co., 1950.

Bridenbaugh, Carl, *Cities in Revolt*. New York: Alfred A. Knopf, 1955.

Carrington, Gen. Henry B., *Battles of the American Revolution*. New York: A. S. Barnes & Co., 1888.

Commager, Henry S. and Morris, Richard B. (Eds.), *The Spirit of 'Seventy-Six*. Indianapolis & New York: The Bobbs-Merrill Co., 1958.

Creasy, Edward S., *The Fifteen Decisive Battles of the World*. New York: A. L. Burt.

Dictionary of American Biography, edited by Allen Johnson. New York: Charles Scribner's Sons, 1943.

Esposito, Col. Vincent J., (Ed.), *The West Point Atlas of American Wars*. New York: Frederick A. Praeger, 1959.

Fisher, Sidney G., *The Struggle for American Independence*. Philadelphia: J. B. Lippincott Co., 1908.

Fiske, John, *The American Revolution*. Boston & New York: Houghton Mifflin Co., 1891.

Fleming, Thomas J., *Now We Are Enemies*. New York: St. Martin's Press, 1960.

Fortescue, Sir John W., *History of the British Army*. London: The Macmillan Co., 1899–1930.

Freeman, Douglas S., *George Washington*. New York: Charles Scribner's Sons, 1948–54.

Frothingham, Capt. Thomas G., *Washington, Commander in Chief*. Boston & New York: Houghton Mifflin Co., 1930.

Fuller, Maj. Gen. J. F. C., *Decisive Battles of the U. S. A.* New York: Thomas Yoseloff, 1942.

Greene, Francis V., *General Greene*. New York: D. Appleton & Co., 1893.

Johnston, Henry P., *The Campaign of 1776 Around New York and Brooklyn*. Brooklyn, New York: Long Island Historical Society, 1878.

———, *The Yorktown Campaign*. New York: Harper & Brothers, 1881.

———, *The Battle of Harlem Heights*. New York: The Macmillan Co., 1897.

Ketcham, Richard M. (Ed.), *The American Heritage Book of the Revolution*. New York: American Heritage Publishing Co., 1958.

Knox, Commodore Dudley W., *A History of the United States Navy*. New York: G. P. Putnam's Sons, 1948.

Lancaster, Bruce, *From Lexington to Liberty*. Garden City, New York: Doubleday & Co., 1955.

Lossing, Benson J., *The Pictorial Field-book of the Revolution*. New York: Harper & Brothers, 1855.

Mahan, Capt. Alfred T., *The Influence of Seapower upon History, 1660–1783*. Boston: Little, Brown & Co., 1890.

——, *Major Operations of the Navies in the War of American Independence*. Boston: Little, Brown & Co., 1913.

Miller, John C., *Triumph of Freedom, 1775–1783*. Boston: Little, Brown & Co., 1948.

Mitchell, Col. William A., *Outlines of the World's Military History*. Washington, D. C.: The Infantry Journal, 1931.

Montross, Lynn, *Rag, Tag and Bobtail*. New York: Harper & Brothers, 1952.

Ogg, Frederic A., *The Old Northwest*. New Haven: Yale University Press, 1919.

Peckham, Howard H., *The War for Independence*. Chicago: The University of Chicago Press, 1958.

Roberts, Kenneth, *The Battle of Cowpens*. New York: Doubleday & Co., 1958.

Scheer, George F. and Rankin, Hugh F., *Rebels and Redcoats*. Cleveland & New York: The World Publishing Co., 1957.

Steele, Maj. Matthew F., *American Campaigns*. Washington, D. C.: Byron S. Adams, 1909.

Trevelyan, Sir George O., *The American Revolution*. London: Longmans, Green & Co., 1921.

Upton, Maj. Gen. Emory, *The Military Policy of the United States*. Washington, D. C.: U. S. Government Printing Office, 1911.

Ward, Christopher, *The War of the Revolution*. New York: The Macmillan Co., 1952.

Wrong, George M., *Washington and His Comrades in Arms*. New Haven: Yale University Press, 1921.

Index

(Ranks given are the highest attained during the war.)